Praise for *The Pen Is Mightier Th.*

In "Behind Julia's Eyes," Barbara Shine muses that "the family playing host to Alzheimer's disease [in her mother-in-law] is rich in opportunities for problem-solving." This hope that order and meaning will emerge from chaos, that new possibilities will rise from what seems intractable, is often reflected in this special collection of autobiographical meditations. In each piece there is always the intention of attention to whatever presents itself to the author's transformative imagination, whether it is a turtle trying to cross a road, the disjointed symphony of a heart murmur, an unremitting depression, or the inadvertent meal of a cockroach. In all, we enjoy the deft touch, the grace of curiosity, and, above all, the love of word following word.

Joseph Mancini, Jr., Ph.D., M.S.O.D., L.C.S.W., D.C.S.W., C.G.P., C.Ht.; Author, instructor, therapist

Poet Denise Levertov writes of the magnetic pull of ancestors: no matter how far afield we wander, we return to writing about our parents. So in discovering one's family, real or adoptive, shoving aside the weeds and boulders, plunging into the wilderness, be it desert or jungle, one may find who one is.

A missing ring, found at the 11th hour, could symbolize many of the pieces in this worthy collection: the retracing of the circle—as if we could find a beginning. For some of these writers—all women with active present lives—the journey is joyous. For others it is painful, downright frightening, as the characters identify the skeletons, literal and figurative, in their closets. Or: liberating. Deep roots can be bitter or nourishing: we are all to some degree "churned in a surf of loss"; but we may also find ourselves "dancing in the blue air."

A beautiful Bulgarian-born mother flees her past to become a pilot in America, a fashion model, and a model Russian émigré. A boisterous St. Patrick's Day parade. A child discovers why her glamorous mother with a dark past and dark skin has made her unacceptable to her new family. Buried memories of an abusive father, other memories of his "surges of creativity and his fury." Through surgery and creativity, we can recreate and hone our lives.

Elisavietta Ritchie, *Flying Time, In Haste I Write You This Note, The Arc of the Storm, Awaiting Permission to Land,* and other books.

The Pen Is Mightier
Than the Broom

To Diane + Leonard —

Barbara Shine

The Pen Is Mightier Than the Broom

Memoirs, Stories, and Poems

By the Stromboli Streghe
Barbara Shine, Editor

iUniverse, Inc.
New York Lincoln Shanghai

The Pen Is Mightier Than the Broom
Memoirs, Stories, and Poems

iUniverse books may be ordered through booksellers or by contacting:

iUniverse
2021 Pine Lake Road, Suite 100
Lincoln, NE 68512
www.iuniverse.com
1-800-Authors (1-800-288-4677)

Cover design by Leon Lawrence III. Cover photograph by David Baratz.

ISBN-13: 978-0-595-41403-1 (pbk)
ISBN-13: 978-0-595-85754-8 (ebk)
ISBN-10: 0-595-41403-6 (pbk)
ISBN-10: 0-595-85754-X (ebk)

Printed in the United States of America

To the Writer's Center, for bringing us together
and nourishing our impulse to write.

Contents

Foreword, by William O'Sullivan xiii

Preface, by Barbara Shine xv

Chapter 1 Before We Knew... 1

    The Birthday, by Julie Link Haifley 3

    Away from harm in the 1930s?, by Nancy Galbraith 5

    My Father's Presence, by Deborah Hefferon 6

    The Ring, by Allyson Denise Walker 6

    Banished Memories (fiction), by Allyson Denise Walker 9

    Prang Crayons, by Julie Link Haifley 9

    Summer 1959, by Julie Link Haifley 19

Chapter 2 Roots and Routes 21

    An Irish Childhood: St. Patrick's Day, by Maria Hogan Pereira 23

    Home, Sweet Home, by Lori Carruthers 23

    Very Far, Very High, by Nancy Galbraith 25

    A Bridge Freshly Tagged, by Ellen Maidman-Tanner 28

    Routes of Escape, by Caroline Cottom 30

Chapter 3 Family Portraits 41

    My Mother's Wings, by Julia Weller 43

    Bonding, by Therese Keane 47

    Portrait of Judge Cook, by Julie Link Haifley 48

    Sister to Sister (fiction), by Allyson Denise Walker 49

    Katherine's Face, by Julie Link Haifley 50

Behind Julia's Eyes, by Barbara Shine 57

For My Daughter, With a Gift of Blue Butterflies for Her Ears,
by Nancy Galbraith 60

Chapter 4 Friends and Other Animals **61**

Coffee Break, by Lori Carruthers 63

Turtle Waltz, by Julia Weller 65

Wave Walking, by Therese Keane 67

Brunching on the Far End of the Food Chain,
by Nancy Galbraith 69

Chapter 5 Body and Soul **71**

Living on Planet Drum, by Barbara Shine 73

Forced Watch, by Barbara Shine 75

Lost Days, by Therese Keane 77

Autism, by Maria Hogan Pereira 78

Seeking the Zen in Bowling, by Lori Carruthers 84

St. Jude and the Tell-Tale Heart, by Barbara Shine 87

Painted Alphabet, by Julie Link Haifley 89

Chapter 6 Candles, Ribbons, and Champagne **91**

Birthday Greetings From New Orleans, by Therese Keane 93

Found Object, by Julia Weller 95

Holiday Blues (fiction), by Allyson Denise Walker 98

Easter Weekend, by Maria Hogan Pereira 106

Sweet Memories, by Lori Carruthers 107

Chapter 7 Falling In, Falling Out **109**

Pergolesi, by Ellen Maidman-Tanner 111

Insight, by Therese Keane 112

Billy (fiction), by Maria Hogan Pereira 113

The Sorrow of Small Losses, by Deborah Hefferon 117

Chapter 8 Beyond the Garden Wall **119**

The Memory of Sound, by Deborah Hefferon 121

The Water, by Caroline Cottom 123

Walking on the Moon, by Julia Weller 124

Ocean Sky, by Therese Keane 124

Unfamiliar Territory, by Deborah Hefferon 128

From a Trip to Egypt, by Ellen Maidman-Tanner 130

Salvador, by Caroline Cottom 132

Chapter 9 Where We've Been **133**

The Fields at Arles, by Caroline Cottom 135

Fall, by Ellen Maidman-Tanner 136

Ghostly Reflections in a Backyard Pool, by Therese Keane 139

Archeology, by Lori Carruthers 141

Up and Down, by Julia Weller................................141

Evening Dresses, by Julie Link Haifley 143

The Contributors **147**

Publication Credits **151**

Foreword

Reading this collection of memoirs, stories, and poems by the Stromboli Streghe is like running into a fondly remembered friend or relative after a long separation. In that unexpected but welcome encounter, certain traits and stories come rushing back—as familiar as a much-heard song—while other inflections and experiences have developed over your time apart. All contribute to the older, ever more interesting figure who stands before you.

Several of these writers met in my personal-essay workshop at the Writer's Center in Bethesda, Maryland, more than 10 years ago. I've taught one or two more of them since then. And a number of names here are new to me, writers whose voices I'm hearing for the first time. As an entity—a body that has grown and changed over a decade—the Stromboli Streghe is that long-lost face on the street, with a lot of new inside her as well. It's a pleasure to see her again.

I always tell my classes at the Writer's Center that one of the greatest things about that wonderful institution—and the writing workshop itself, no matter where you find it—is the community it creates, both during those eight weeks we're together and, for some, in the years that follow. The people you meet in a writing class can be portable, an ever-replenishing picnic of creative sustenance and support. If you're a writer, you need to hold tight to fellow storytellers and to rigorous, smart, sympathetic critics who will continue to nourish your desire to put words on paper. Writers need encouragement more than anything else.

So here's to the Stromboli Streghe for 10 years—and many more—of encouraging words. Those words represent real lives, and nothing is more precious than that.

William O'Sullivan

"By the way, does anything other than 'trouble' rhyme with 'bubble'?"

Preface

Come inside these pages and meet the women of Stromboli Streghe, who proclaim, "The pen is mightier than the broom"; and find out what that statement means to them.

More than 10 years ago, in 1994, a half-dozen women in a workshop led by Joe Mancini at the Writer's Center in Bethesda, Maryland, decided to meet on their own when the workshop ended. The women, ages ranging from 25 to 65, shared a passion for creative nonfiction, mainly the personal essay, and wanted to continue meeting in a critique group. They would come together twice a month at Stromboli's, a café around the corner from the Writer's Center, to share what they had written, learn from each other, and hone their skills. They wanted to publish their work, and most had never done so.

Charter members of the group took part in further workshops, benefiting from the wealth of skills and knowledge shared by Writer's Center instructors such as Bill O'Sullivan, Joanna Biggar, William Loiseaux, Anne Becker, Sara Tabor, Barbara Esstman, Martin Galvin, and Liz Polliner. (A couple of the Streghe have followed these strong models to become workshop leaders themselves.) More workshops produced not only better writing, but also more prospective group members. I was honored by an invitation to join when I met Caroline Cottom and Nancy Galbraith in the first of several Bill O'Sullivan personal-essay workshops that I attended.

As time passed, new members joined us, and some left the group: We lost them to distant graduate schools or new jobs in other states or to different writing goals. No one left for lack of interest. Our meetings were always greatly anticipated and rewarding. And the good people at Stromboli's demonstrated a high tolerance for our table-hogging and, usually, coffee-only patronage.

The group grew and shrank but maintained a steady six to eight members, and we quickly began to see tangible results from the critique-and-revision formula we developed. We held our collective breath after essay submissions went into the mail. Then we celebrated with giddy excitement—and sometimes a Stromboli's pizza—when our writings appeared in the *Washington Post, Christian Science Monitor,* and *Common Boundary Magazine,* and in such literary journals as *Potomac Review, Iris, The Sun,* and *WordWrights!* Each submitted work was a cosseted offspring of the group, and each published piece was pride and joy for us all.

Soon we began to think about giving a reading to share our successes with the Writer's Center community. But how would we bill ourselves? We needed a name for the group: Of course, it would include "Stromboli," for our meeting place, but then what? The "Streghe"—Italian for "witches"—were born after just a brief labor. As our footing and writings had grown stronger, so had our sense of power: We thought of ourselves as "word witches," using the wizardry that grew out of group chemistry to transform ideas into powerful prose.

We also invented a slogan, "The pen is mightier than the broom," and proclaimed it on brilliant turquoise T-shirts printed for our first reading. We wanted all to know that writer-women have strength beyond what it takes to push—or fly—a broom. The Streghe offered several readings at the Writer's Center over the next few years.

At the 10-year mark, in 2004, when we decided to produce this collection, the Stromboli Streghe were seven women strong and still evolving. Some of our newer members are writers of primarily short fiction, and one of our charter members is finishing her first novel. Creative nonfiction is still important in the group, and we all take a swipe at poetry from time to time.

Our anthology gives you a glimpse into our Saturday gatherings over the years, since some of the boxed "short takes" sprinkled throughout the book grew out of timed-writing exercises, which follow relaxation breathing at every meeting. We also offer here some of the best concoctions to pour out of our cauldron in the past 10 to 12 years, true stories and fiction and poems.

Many of these works have been published; some have not yet found their niche in the wider world. But even if we haven't touched you with a Streghe spell, it's likely you'll find something here to enjoy.

Barbara Shine

Chapter 1

Before We Knew...

The Birthday
By Julie Link Haifley

Today I am wearing my new plaid skirt and white blouse with matching trim and new blue Keds, my first ones this spring. I walk across my backyard toward the shortcut through the Dentons' yard and I can smell honeysuckle on the back hedge when Miss Roller calls, "Ju-lie, come back here." She wants to tell me something that I don't want to hear. She is a stupid old babysitter who doesn't know anything except what Mama tells her. But she's the boss while Mama's gone, so I have to go back.

This is what I know: Mama had her little brown suitcase packed for the last two weeks. Aunt Alice gave her a fancy pink nightgown and matching robe that she put in the suitcase along with a Frank Yerby book, some notepaper, and her favorite pen. Last night Daddy took Mama to the hospital in the middle of the night because she's having *another* baby. She has probably had it by now. I don't care whether it's a boy or a girl. I already have one younger brother and sister. That's enough!

I might as well tell you why I'm so cross. I am 8 years old; in fact, *exactly* 8 years old today. Isn't it bad enough that she's having another baby? Now she has to have it on *my* birthday! Everyone will be so excited about the new baby; they will forget all about *me*. And Mama won't be home in time to bake my favorite chocolate cake. Just thinking about that cake makes my mouth water.

Here is what I don't know: *Why* is Mama having another baby? Can she help it or does it just happen? I think it has something to do with Mama and Daddy sleeping in the same bed, but I don't know for sure. My cousin Jana, who has four brothers and sisters, told me that our parents do yucky things together to make a baby, but I don't believe her. Miss Roller told me a silly story about a stork at breakfast. How could a *bird* bring a real live baby to the hospital? If it could fly to the hospital, why couldn't it just fly to our house instead and land on our porch? Then Mama wouldn't have to go to the hospital in the middle of the night to get the baby. Mama and Daddy's hurried voices and the back screen slamming woke me up last night, but I was too sleepy to get up and wave good-bye.

Well, back to my birthday. I turn around and walk slowly across the yard past our jungle gym to the back door where Miss Roller is waiting for me. She is wearing the ugliest blue-flowered dress you have ever seen with black lace-up shoes and white socks. She has a big grin on her Moon-pie face. *Please, please don't tell me*. Of course she does: "You have a new baby sister!" As if that is the greatest news in the world.

I start to feel sick to my stomach. I don't know what to say, so I hug the book-bag to my chest and bow my head, staring at my Keds. Finally I just say, "I'm going to be late for school if I don't go now." Before Miss Roller can say another word, I turn around and walk away, past our tree swing with the bare spot underneath and the empty sandbox where my brother teased me with live caterpillars when we were little. I am almost to the Dentons' hedge again before I feel warm tears on my cheeks. I wipe them away with the back of my hand and sing to myself all the way to school, "Happy birthday to me…happy birthday to me…"

Away from harm in the 1930s?
By Nancy Galbraith

Stuck piano keys got worse
and wood swelled fat in cabin
doorways those summers
at Camp Sleepaway where

you might get tossed flat
off a bay gelding called "Snockers,"
and at archery you could miss
your target, hit a rock, break
your arrow—and Campfire Night

your marshmallow could slither
to the cinders off the slender
bending willow switch you'd cut,

but, stashed in those woods by your
folks, you couldn't—

because maybe it came from
peach pits
or maybe from swimming
pools
or maybe from grapefruit
skins
or maybe from your town's
movie house
you couldn't
in this sylvan world
catch polio.

My Father's Presence
By Deborah Hefferon

October 1953

Wednesday. Grandmom comes on Wednesdays. Now it's fall and my brother, Dennis, is in morning kindergarten and I have Grandmom all to myself. I am almost 3 years old on this cool October morning. I wait on the front porch of our house in Olney, Philadelphia. I sit on the phone book placed on top of the wooden stool with the embroidered cushion so I can see through the screen when Grandmom comes down the street. Waiting takes such a long time. Dennis will be home if she doesn't come soon. What will she bring me? I see her white head coming down Front Street. I see the Lit Brothers shopping bag swinging from her white glove. It must be full of wonderful things. "Grandmom's here!"

"Come on out back. I wanna get a picture before it clouds up again. 'Morning, Mother. You look so nice in that blue coat. I love that coat."

Mommy loves me, too. Grandmom takes my hand and we follow Mommy all the way through the house.

The Ring

There it was, lying on the maroon velvet bottom of my jewelry box—the opal ring Grandma Jean had given me when I was 10. She was so disappointed in me when it turned up missing a year later that she gave her strand of real pearls to my cousin Jenell, who was two years older. Jenell wore those pearls to her prom and every other formal occasion since, even for her wedding.

Grandma Jean eventually forgave me for losing the ring, but she never gave me another piece of jewelry. I still had her manual typewriter, the one I'd used to type all my college papers. And now here was the ring. Why did I find it today?

I slipped the ring on my finger as I heard Mama calling; the limo was waiting. Mama stood at the foot of the stairs in the black linen dress she'd worn to every funeral she'd attended in the past 10 years. I ran down and held out my hand. She took it and looked into my face, her eyes filling. It was her lap I'd soaked with my tears after confessing the loss of the ring to Grandma Jean.

"It must have been hidden in my jewelry box all these years. Why did I have to find it now?" I asked.

Mama managed a trembly smile. "Maybe it's her way of saying good-bye."

—Allyson Denise Walker

In her other hand she carries the bag. As we pass the green velvet sofa, she drops it on the lumpy cushion. In the summer it's too hot to sit there. "Sticky," we say when we sit there. The living room is jammed with small tables that are crowded with things I'm not allowed to touch: china dolls and bells and cups and souvenirs from the Poconos and Atlantic City. Grandmom asks, "What are these called, Debbie?"

"Knock-knocks," I say, and she laughs. A tiny laugh like bubbles bursting or baby hiccups.

"Knickknacks," she instructs, and we both laugh. My laugh is loud and it hurts my stomach.

On the corner window sill is the record player that I can pile 45s on, but I have to wait until Daddy pushes the red button for them to drop and play. Sometimes two drop at once and he says, "Shit." Sometimes he picks me up and we dance to "High Hopes" and Mommy says, "Be careful of the table...the lamp...the vase." Tsk-tsk, she always says when I'm in Daddy's arms. Tsk-tsk.

The dining room is dark and cool and filled with the big mahogany table that I'm not allowed to get finger prints on and the eight matching chairs Mommy calls the good chairs. I'm good, too. We can eat here when we have company, and at Christmas our tree that touches the ceiling lives here and the train platform with the little trees covered with snow that never melts.

I jump from the dining room carpet to the black and white tile kitchen floor. The refrigerator hums. I can hum, too. I pull away from Grandmom's hand and scramble onto the red leather booth where we eat Cheerios, morning snack, lunch, afternoon snack, dinner, ice cream for dessert. Some days, if it's really hot, we eat our peanut butter and jelly sandwiches and iced tea on the front porch and it's so wonderful. "Maybe we can catch a breeze," Mommy always says. I catch lightning bugs sometimes.

"Debbie, come here!" The screen door slams and Grandmom helps me down the back stairs. Be careful on the last step because it's broken and Daddy's never home to fix it.

"Does she need a coat?" Mommy yells from the spot where my pool used to be. Grandmom shakes her head no. I shake my head too, and Grandmom laughs her little laugh.

"Sit still," Mommy yells.

We are sitting on the white wooden bench at the corner by the Braxton's yard next to the little white fence that makes a circle around Daddy's garden. It used to smell like onions but now it smells like dirt. I lean over the fence and see long vines like jumping ropes covering the ground.

"Watermelon!" I cry.

"Honey, sit still." I can smell Grandmom's lily of the valley perfume when she leans over me. "I'll give you a candy if you sit still. Wait a minute, Dorothy," Grandmom yells to Mommy.

Out of her pocket comes a black and gold tin. I try to help her open it but my fingernails are too short and round and white. Grandmom's are pink like my nightgown. She opens the tin with her thumbnail and inside are tiny purple candies that smell like lavender. "Sen-Sen," she tells me and I think that I will call my new doll Sen-Sen. I hope Grandmom brought me a new doll today.

"New dolly!" I squeal as Grandmom puts two pieces of Sen-Sen in my mouth. They taste like flowers. They are so small that they keep disappearing under my tongue and behind my teeth.

"Mother, make her sit still!"

Grandmom puts her arm around my back and whispers, "Now, smile."

"Say cheese," Mommy says.

"Lunch," I shout, and I swing my feet to jump off the bench. The camera blinks at me and Grandmom.

Banished Memories (fiction)
By Allyson Denise Walker

Nan was late picking me up from gymnastics. A fine, misty rain was falling in the twilight, so all the cars driving past had their lights on. I stood in the doorway, gym bag on my arm and book bag at my feet, waiting for Nan. A lot of cars were pulled over to the curb, mothers coming to pick up their daughters, but no one for me. Some of the girls said, "Bye" and "See you later," as they passed me on their way out. I responded absently, focusing on the street. Nan rarely kept me waiting.

After a while, the gym emptied and the lights went out one by one. I let the gym bag slide off my arm and pressed my forehead against the glass pane next to the door. It started raining harder, making it difficult to see the cars passing in the dusk. All I could make out were white headlights and red brake lights.

"Melanie? Your mom isn't here yet?" Ginny, the gymnastics instructor, was headed in my direction.

"No," I said, but just then a car pulled up and the horn honked.

I let out a deep breath. "There she is." I pulled up my hood and grabbed my bags.

Prang Crayons

Prang. That harsh sound conjures up a flat, black-and-white box the size of my red plastic autograph book. The edges of the box are crisp and smooth; I know that soon they will become softened with use, like velvet or suede. I open the lid and sniff the aroma of brand-new crayons. Beginnings: a new school year and a new teacher whom I will come to love, or merely tolerate. I wonder if she will like me. Will I be her pet this year? Nervous butterflies in my tummy might override my excitement, but the anticipation of using the crayons to color worksheets, draw letters and shapes wins out. Then come the pure physical sensations of sight and smell: perfect points, waxy, delicious. If I could eat them, they would color my insides brilliant primary and secondary colors. The black one would outline all the shapes and connect them to each other like dot-to-dots in an activity book. They would feel firm and slightly crunchy, the texture of a Hershey bar. Mmmmm.

Carefully, I arrange the crayons in rainbow order from left to right with the black and brown ones on the right side of the box. I am eager to make a scribbled design, fill in the irregular spaces with color, then cover the page with shiny black strokes before scratching my real picture through the top layer. But that project will have to wait. For now, I close my eyes and savor the first day of school.

—Julie Link Haifley

Ginny smiled. "See you next week."

I pushed the door open and hurried out into the rain. "Bye."

Nan wasn't driving. She sat on the passenger side and my father was behind the wheel. I wanted to turn around and run back into the gym. Instead I pulled my hood closer, walked over and crawled into the back seat, and shut the door.

"I'm sorry I'm late, but your father wanted to go straight to your grandmother's tonight instead of leaving in the morning," Nan explained.

"That's okay," I lied, settling in my seat.

"How did you do on your chemistry test?" she asked.

"89."

"That'll bring your average down, won't it?"

"Only to a 91."

Nan sighed. I thought it was because of my chemistry grade, but she said, "Oh, Frank, I don't see why we can't get a second car. A used one wouldn't be as expensive as a new one."

"I'm not spending a dime on another car for you. You already have a car to drive."

"But that's your car, and whenever you want to drive it, I have to depend on you to get where I need to go."

"I take the train to work every day so you can drive my car. You *have* a car to drive."

"But when you start this new job you're going to need the car with you. How will I get Melanie back and forth to school?"

"Let her ride the school bus."

"But Frank, you know I hate to have Melanie exposed to that bus environment. So many of those kids come from inner-city neighborhoods, and I think they're a bit rough."

"Don't forget she came from that environment before she ended up with me," snapped my father.

"Don't forget it's *your* daughter I'm hauling back and forth," countered Nan, her voice rising. She must have forgotten I was sitting right behind her.

I pulled my feet up under me and leaned against the car door, trying not to listen. I closed my eyes and pretended to be asleep, not bothering to brush away the two tears that slid down my cheeks. I knew how to be invisible when I needed to be.

*   *   *

Every Thanksgiving since I was 6 and went to live with my father, he took us to Grandmother's for dinner. Before then, I'd lived with "Mama Lucy," my other grandmother, in the upstairs rooms of a tiny bungalow that had been my entire world. I knew where to avoid playing marbles so they wouldn't roll into the cracks in the floor, where to put the pots to catch the water when it rained, and where I could hide candy in the hole behind the sofa. Mama Lucy had spent most of her time cooking and keeping other children, whom I hid from, mostly. Then she went to the hospital and didn't come back, and the next thing I knew I was in church.

Mama Lucy's funeral and my father's wedding to Nan ran together in my memory.

That first Thanksgiving at Grandmother's I was so overwhelmed by everything I could hardly speak. She has one of those big country homes with a vast yard. Her furniture always seems like new, almost too good to sit on.

The first time Grandmother saw me she said, "Come here, child. Let me get a good look at you." I walked up to her chair slowly. She peered down into my face with icy gray eyes and said, "She's a little dark, Francis. She looks just like her mother."

I didn't understand what she meant by that. I just knew that she didn't reach out and pull me to her with, "Give Grandma some sugar," as Mama Lucy used to. It wasn't until later that I discovered how I could be brown in a family where everyone else was fair and light-eyed. I didn't remember my mother, who had died when I was a baby, but Mama Lucy had told me that she'd been a woman of incredible beauty and that I took after her. So I was not ashamed.

The week that Grandmother kept me while my father and Nan went on vacation to the Bahamas was one of the most miserable I've ever spent. I was 12 at the time and self-conscious about my body beginning to curve in and out like a woman's. I'd tried to be modest and undress in the bathroom, but one night Grandmother caught me.

"Look at you," she snapped. "Growing up mighty fast, aren't you? I'll bet you like the boys already, too."

Actually, I was terrified of them. "No, ma'am."

"It's shameful. A girl your age poking out in front like that. Don't think I haven't noticed, either. Nan doesn't know how to handle girls like you, but I know how to keep you out of trouble."

She went to the linen closet, pulled out a white sheet, and ripped it neatly. I watched her hands, old-lady hands, but strong. I watched her fingers sinking into my flesh as she squeezed my arm. "Take off that bra and turn around." I did, and she bound my breasts with that sheet.

Later on when I told Nan about it, she was upset, but she never mentioned it. No one dared to cross Grandmother. I never liked going to see her after that, but we had to do the Thanksgiving visit or she'd be offended.

This Thanksgiving I managed to avoid Grandmother by staying in the guest room reading all morning, until Nan arrived at my doorway.

"Melanie, Aunt Barbara and Uncle Lloyd are here with Tish," she said. I shut my book and followed her downstairs.

We walked into the family room, where Uncle Henry and Uncle Lloyd were watching a football game on television. They each stood up to give me a brief hug and then went back to the game. I sat in a chair, but Nan said, "Melanie, why don't you go play with Tish?"

"I haven't seen her," I said, looking up.

"She's in the kitchen with her mother," Uncle Lloyd said.

I got up and went into the kitchen. Tish was already sitting at the table, reading *Essence* magazine. Aunt Barbara and Grandmother were bent in front of the oven, trying to make room for one more foil-covered casserole dish. I sat down at the table and said, "Hi, Tish."

She looked up from her magazine. "Oh, hi, Melanie," she said and went back to reading.

I tried again. "Any good articles in there?"

"Yeah." Tish put the magazine down and examined her mauve fingernails. She looks like Lisa Bonet from the "Cosby Show," but she dresses like a fashion magazine. We're both 15, but she acts like she's 20.

"Melanie, how's school coming?" Aunt Barbara asked.

"Oh, fine."

"Are you still taking piano lessons?" she asked as Nan came into the kitchen. Nan and Aunt Barbara had been friends from college, although I couldn't see why. All they seemed to do these days was play "my daughter is better than your daughter."

"Of course she's still taking piano lessons," Nan said. I traced the embossed floral pattern in the salmon tablecloth, wishing she'd stayed in the living room.

"I suppose she keeps you busy," said Aunt Barbara.

Nan gave a little laugh, and I knew she had that same expression on her face that she gets when she looks in the mirror just before going out and likes what she sees. "Melanie has such an exhausting schedule: Violin lessons on Mondays and Thursdays, piano on Tuesdays, gymnastics on Wednesdays, SAT preparation on Saturday mornings, and youth orchestra on Saturday afternoons."

"That's quite a schedule," Aunt Barbara remarked. "But isn't it too early to worry about SATs?"

"She took them in the summer and scored under 1200, so she wants to take them over. Of course, we're not going to send her off to college now, but in case she wants to go later on," Nan finished up, leaving Aunt Barbara to be properly shocked at my progress. I wasn't looking at Tish but I could feel her radiating hostility in my direction.

"What grade are you in?" my aunt asked.

"The academy is ungraded," began Nan, before I could open my mouth, "but she tested 12th year."

"That's excellent, Nan," Aunt Barbara said with a glance at me, "but when does Melanie have time to have any fun? I'm sure she'd love to go to one of Tish's parties."

I bit my lip, knowing Tish would die of embarrassment if she had to take me to one of her parties.

"I don't let Melanie run around with just anyone," Nan said, "and she has lots of fun at orchestra and gymnastics; don't you, Melanie?" She gave me a meaningful stare. I gave Aunt Barbara a small smile.

"At least you could let us take her to the mall for some new clothes," Aunt Barbara persisted. "Wouldn't you like that, Melanie?"

"She has plenty of new clothes," Nan cut in. It was true. I had a closet full of clothes, but none of them looked like the outfits in *Seventeen*. All of the tops were high in the neck, all of the skirts fell below the knee, and nothing fit to my figure. In this, Nan and I agreed. We both found it easier to hide my shape when we shopped for clothes.

"Well, at least Melanie is a well-rounded girl," Aunt Barbara remarked, retreating. "All Tish cares about is makeup and boys." I looked up at Tish then and made an exasperated face. She rolled her eyes.

"They're such different girls," responded Nan.

Tish leaned over and whispered to me. "Want to try on my makeup?"

I grinned in relief. "Sure."

We left the kitchen table and went upstairs to the bathroom. Tish made me stand with my back to the mirror so I couldn't see what she was doing.

"You've got great eyelashes," she remarked.

I said, "Mm-hmm," because she was working with the lipstick brush.

"Okay. Turn around."

I did. I saw an improvement, and I looked a little older.

"Do you think I look like my mother?" I asked.

"I've never seen your mother. Have you ever made out with a boy before?"

"No," I said, still examining my reflection.

"It figures."

The door opened and Nan poked her head in. "Girls, it's time—." She stopped and pushed the door further. "What's going on?"

"Tish offered to give me a makeover."

Nan grabbed a jar of cold cream and reached for the tissues. "Young lady, did I give you permission to wear makeup?"

I started backing away from her and bumped into Tish. "Oh, please don't be mad at me. I only did it to see if I'm going to be as pretty as my mother."

"Well, you're not." She took hold of my chin and started swiping at my face. "And you're not to wear makeup until I say you can."

I clenched my teeth, but tears ran into the tissue as Nan rubbed at my skin. "For heaven's sake, don't cry. It's so childish." She threw the tissue into the wastebasket. "Now wash up and come down to dinner."

Nan left, and Tish looked me up and down with a glance that was a mixture of pity and disgust, then followed Nan out the door. I stood looking in the mirror for a moment, then bent down and sobbed into my handful of cold water.

*   *   *

I made it through dinner without being noticed. As I watched everyone talking and laughing, I kept waiting for the familiar feeling of comfort that being invisible usually brought me. It never came. Instead, I felt great waves of loneliness that settled like a lump in my throat and made the food seem dry and tasteless.

The minute the meal was over, I stood up and began collecting plates. Aunt Barbara commented on how well-mannered I'd become, but I disappeared into the kitchen to avoid seeing Nan's self-satisfied smile and Tish's narrow-eyed scowl.

"You don't have to do this all yourself," said Aunt Barbara, bringing more dishes from the table.

"I don't mind," I said, carefully rinsing and stacking the plates. Grandmother never put her fine china in the dishwasher.

Aunt Barbara set her dishes down, put her cheek against mine, and squeezed my arms. I leaned against her for a moment and had to swallow hard before I could speak.

"Aunt Barbara," I began, after she'd stepped away, "do you remember my mother?"

She bent down and rummaged through a cabinet. "I'm afraid I don't remember your mother very well, Melanie."

"But what do you remember?"

She gave a quick glance toward the door. "Well, let's see. She was beautifully dressed and an excellent seamstress. She made all her own clothes."

"Really?" I made up my mind to ask Nan if I could take sewing, even though it wasn't a college prep elective.

Aunt Barbara gave me a smile. "Yes," she said slowly. "And she sang beautifully."

"Was she in the choir at church?"

"Well...no.... She didn't exactly sing in church." Aunt Barbara's face disappeared behind the counter as she searched for more containers for the leftovers.

I caught my breath. "You mean she sang on stage?"

Aunt Barbara concentrated on filling a plastic bowl with stuffing. "She sang in...actually, she sang in nightclubs, mostly."

"Oh." I imagined my mother on a nightclub stage like Diana Ross in "Lady Sings the Blues."

"Aunt Barbara, did she...did she love me?"

She looked up sharply, and then her eyes filled with tears. "Of course she loved you! She loved you very much, and don't you ever forget it!" She went back to filling containers with candied yams and green beans with more force than they needed.

I stood by the sink, clutching a glass, my knees shaking, unable to stop myself from asking, "How did she die?"

"Oh, Melanie, I don't think..."

"My whole life no one will ever tell me how she died, and she was my mother," I said quietly and clearly.

At that moment the swinging kitchen doors parted, and Grandmother stepped in. She flashed her furious eyes from Aunt Barbara to me. "Don't you *ever* mention that woman in my house again!" She hissed, her words coiling like a whip about to strike. The glass I was holding slipped from my fingers and shattered on the floor.

"I—I'm sorry," I stammered, staring at the glass shards on the floor in horror.

Aunt Barbara grabbed a broom and dustpan from the corner and rushed toward me.

"You should be sorry!" snapped Grandmother.

Her words smacked me in the chest and I flinched. I hated having an apology thrown back in my face.

"I am sorry," I heard myself repeat. "Do you want me to pay for the glass out of my allowance?"

"I don't want your money," she spat. "And I have more than a dozen glasses. I want you out of my sight. Now!"

I wanted to run but stood rooted to the spot. Instead, I burst into tears. Misery poured through me, and I shook with sobs, my tears splashing on the floor.

"Mother! She's just a girl!" Aunt Barbara was crouched down on the floor at my feet, sweeping broken glass into the dustpan. She stood up and faced Grandmother.

"She's not a girl any longer, more's the pity. Just look at that figure. She's a junior-grade slut. How can you look at her and not be reminded?"

"She is not!" Nan shrieked. I glanced up to see everyone crowding into the kitchen. "She is nothing like her mother; I've made sure of that!"

Something in my chest snapped. "Is that why you all hate me?" I screamed. "Because I look like my mother? Well, I can't help the way I look, and I don't even know what my mother did to make you hate her so much, because no one will tell me! No one will tell me and she was *my mother!*" I yelled through my tears.

Grandmother inhaled sharply then snapped her mouth into a thin line. "Your mother was little better than a whore. She slept her way into this family by getting pregnant with you, and she died in a car accident running around with another man!"

"Enough!" my father yelled, his face purple, a vein jumping in his temple. "Whatever she was, she was my wife, and if you have any respect for me, you won't discuss her!"

"I'll show you all the respect you showed me when you took up with her in the first place. I told you not to mess with her, but once she seduced you, you wouldn't listen. You put your own needs before your family name and look what it brought you. You brought shame on this family. You deserve no better than to have this girl in your house as a constant reminder of it!"

One look at my father's face showed me she was telling the truth.

I was trembling all over, and tears still poured down my face, but I was angry enough to make my voice calm. "You're a nasty, mean old woman. You can't stand the sight of me because I remind you of my mother, and you don't even have enough heart to love me for me!" I stood there, fists clenched at my sides. "And now I can't stand you!"

Grandmother crossed the room in three strides and slapped me hard across the face. "You ungrateful girl! How dare you talk to me like that!" She turned to my father. "You take her away from here and never bring her back again."

"If this child isn't welcome in your house, then neither am I." Aunt Barbara spoke quietly but firmly.

"Then not a penny of my money will you get when I die," Grandmother said through clenched teeth. Aunt Barbara didn't flinch.

Nan spoke up. "I've done my best by Melanie and I'm proud of her even if you aren't," she said, sending a brief smile in my direction. "If you won't have her in your home, then I need not come back, either."

"I wouldn't have you," countered Grandmother. "The only reason Frank offered to marry you was to care for the girl, and you were so desperate for a husband, you accepted."

Nan's mouth fell open, but no words came out.

Grandmother looked over her sons and daughters by birth and marriage and her grandchildren. "All of you can get out! Grandfather and I worked hard for the money to put you all through school and earn the respect this family seems to take for granted today. We have a position to uphold in this community that is more important than indulging in selfish desires. Just remember, you are what you are today because of me and what I've sacrificed. I would have expected more gratitude than this." She pushed her way through the small crowd and disappeared through the swinging doors.

I caught my father's eye. "Do you hate me because I remind you of my mother, too?"

He eyed me without expression. "I would rather not be reminded of her and what she did." He turned on this heel and left, also. After an awkward pause, the uncles glanced uncomfortably around the room and followed.

I turned to Aunt Barbara. "Is it true? What she said about my mother?"

She opened her mouth, then shut it and sighed. "There was talk," she said finally. "And your Uncle Lloyd did tell me that she approached him about a divorce. I think she was unhappy with your father."

I studied the linoleum and didn't say anything.

"Lloyd said he told her that she might have a custody battle on her hands if she filed for divorce," Aunt Barbara went on. "He said she was torn because she wanted to leave Frank but didn't want to risk losing you."

I slowly raised my eyes. "You aren't just saying that, are you?"

She shook her head. "You can ask your uncle."

I looked at Nan. "I've disappointed you, haven't I?"

She pressed her lips together, eyes filling with tears. "You haven't ever disappointed me," she said in a trembling voice, coming over to pull me into her arms. I couldn't remember her ever hugging me that close.

*   *   *

We cleaned up Grandmother's kitchen and divided up most of the leftovers. Nan let me go home with Aunt Barbara and Uncle Lloyd so I could spend the rest of the weekend with Tish. Aunt Barbara and Tish took me to the beauty shop to have my hair done and then to the mall to buy me some clothes as an early Christmas present.

"You look okay when you're not trying to dress like a 10-year-old," said Tish with grudging admiration as we dressed for a party later that evening.

"Thanks." I grinned at her reflection in the mirror as Aunt Barbara tapped on the door and stuck her head in.

"Melanie? I have something for you." She handed me a photograph. "I found this picture of your mother last night, and I thought you'd like to have it."

I stared at it for a long while. She was as beautiful as everyone had said, even without the light complexion everyone in the family admired. Her shoulder-length hair flipped up at the ends and she wore a sleeveless black minidress. Her style reminded me of the Supremes. And her face...it was almost like the face I saw in the mirror every morning.

I looked up at Aunt Barbara. "Thank you," I said softly. Then, carefully so as not to crumple the picture, I gave her a hug.

She let go and glanced over my shoulder. "Tish, come and see a picture of Melanie's mother."

Tish was sticking her head out of the doorway. She came all the way out and stood on my other side to see the picture. "She's fantastic," she said. "A little too '60s, maybe, but...Mel, if you wore your hair like that, you'd look just like her. Want me to flip the ends?"

"That's okay, Tish," I said. "Maybe next time."

Summer 1959
By Julie Link Haifley

Blue formica brimming light
Fan blades whirring
     whitest noise

Steam clouds rising, ears of corn
Gray-green beans, transparent grease
Vermillion garden globes sliced round

Metallic trays of frozen shards
Crystal tumblers embracing tea
Pungent whiffs: Vidalia, mint

Ponytail feathers slender neck
Naked feet, insouciant breeze
Breastbuds grazing cotton ground

Sweaty fingers riffling leaves
Transporting one to realms unknown
Lingering pleasures: Body, soul.

Chapter 2

Roots and Routes

An Irish Childhood: St. Patrick's Day
By Maria Hogan Pereira

Finally it would arrive, one of the best days of the year, St. Patrick's Day. It was a great respite after three to four weeks of the deprivations of Lent: All the sweets we could eat, a parade, and a trip to the Silver Swan afterward with Mum and Dad. Who cared if it would freeze the balls of a brass monkey? Weren't Easter and good weather just around the corner?

Best of all, St. Patrick was ours. He belonged just to us, uniquely Irish.

Everybody had St. Patrick's Day off except the publicans and a few of the sweet shop and paper shop owners. We were up early because it was a Mass day. Daddy would go out to pick a clump of shamrock to put on his and Mum's coat lapels. Our St. Patrick's day badges—green rosettes with gold letters proclaiming the day—were all ready to wear; we had lovingly chosen them a few weeks earlier in Nan O'Brien's shop.

After our tea and boiled eggs, off we'd go to 10:30 Mass at St. Joseph's Cathedral, thankful this day's Mass was never too long. The highlight was the singing of our special hymn, "Hail Glorious St. Patrick," at the end. It was such an uplifting tune, even for those who didn't sing. How happy I felt as the lovely hymn resounded off the high cathedral walls!

As everybody poured out of the cathedral, there was a rush to get down to town and find a good spot to see the parade. Our first stop, though, was Clare O'Boyle's, to blow our allowances on all the sweets we had been deprived of since Lent began.

The parade itself was always a delight, but only after the new cars from the local dealerships were gone. One after the other they would drone by with their proud owners waving from the drivers' seats like royalty. The highlights of the parade were the marching bands and the floats. The bands came from all over the country, and they

Home, Sweet Home

Bred and fed in middle America, I spiced my food with salt, pepper, and poultry seasoning. Holiday meals featured molded Jell-O topped with miniature marshmallows. Leaving home, I traveled the seven continents for work and pleasure, seeking the exotic in food and adventure. In Africa, my meals were supplemented with manioc leaves, properly cooked to avoid cyanide poisoning. I refused monkey meat but found it true that alligator tastes like chicken. Cloves bought in Malawi sit next to cardamom from India in my Maryland kitchen. It was cinnamon-sugared toast that made me feel at home in Kiribati.

—Lori Carruthers

varied from schoolchildren in simple uniforms to grownups dressed in kilts, sashes, and big furry hats. Of course there were Irish dancers galore in their colorful costumes, long before "Riverdance" came into being. Fire trucks and ambulances were also shown, but the floats were the thing: Every year there were three contenders for the grand prize—the Electric Supply Board, the Post Office, and the Gowna Wood Industries plant in Collooney. How we looked forward to them! And they never disappointed, with their parodies of political situations and TV programs and ad campaigns.

After the parade everybody headed for their favorite pub for hot whiskeys to warm up. St. Patrick's Day was always cold. Mum and Dad's favorite place was the Silver Swan Hotel on Hyde Bridge. We kids could run around and up and down the stairs while the grownups drank and chatted. Daddy would usually move on to pints of Guinness, while Mum's beverage in those long-ago days was Babycham, a pretend champagne made from pear juice. We kids guzzled Club Orange, Fanta orange, apple-flavored Cidona, and any other fizzy concoction we could get our hands on.

St. Paddy's day had the same pub hours as Sunday, so at about 2:30 we would head home for dinner, the mid-day meal. What a dinner it was: Mum would turn the lamb on at a low heat in the morning before we headed out for the festivities, so we would arrive home to the tempting aroma of succulent lamb. The roast was accompanied by mashed carrots and parsnips, peas, and mash potatoes. For dessert we would have trifle as well as a green-and-white-iced sponge cake in honor of the occasion. Mum always bought such cakes at the bakery, as she had no electric mixer.

The rest of St. Patrick's Day we spent trying to eat more sweets and deal with our full stomachs. Daddy would take a second jaunt to the pub after tea in the evening, and we children would go to our beds more than ready to resume our frugal Lenten habits the next day.

Very Far, Very High
By Nancy Galbraith

I have just slept soundly, and alone, lost under a good duvet of air and goose down. I am 25 and farther away from home than I have ever been before.

It is late March and cold here, the end of the winter skiing. I am in a south-facing room with French doors and a little white iron balcony, halfway up a medium-heavy Alp called the Rigi, and this is the Grand Hotel, Rigi Kaltbad.

Not skiing, I am here for only several days to rest before I go in the old creaking and clanking electric train down this steep mountain to Vitznau at the lakeshore, cross Lake Lucerne by tour boat, then steam by train to Zurich for my plane back to Boston and the man I will decide, a year from now, to marry.

I will come all this way partly to think things over, partly for the lark of getting away from thinking about anything. I am the ski-free member of a 13-day bargain ski charter, and everybody else is on some other mountain.

It is just after first light. I am sitting bolt upright in the middle of a big bed. I am wearing a fur coat and waiting for breakfast.

On my tray will be fresh warm croissants, sweet butter, a small pot of bittersweet marmalade, a day-old air-edition *N.Y. Trib*, a white pot of hot black coffee with its squat sidekick, the little white jug of hot milk. My sturdy black leather shoes are out in the hall, and I will soon find them there, shined and not swiped. For trudging in the snow today and tomorrow I will borrow boots from the hotel.

I have slept naked, but put on the fur coat to honor Swiss formality and my waiter. When I packed, the Elf of Packing, close pal of the Muse of Comedy, assured me it would be silly—no, redundant—to bring both a fur coat *and* a bathrobe all the way to Europe! Bathrobe occasions could be handled in a fur coat, as when, barefooting it coat-clad down a hotel hallway last week in Florence seeking a tub bath, I passed the great Italian actress Anna Magnani, also barefoot, crunching along from our common bathroom on feet as big as planks, wearing a huge mink coat down to her ankles. A sight to treasure.

The coat in which I await breakfast is a surprise birthday present from my mother. In my last college term, she brought it by train to my bedside in the infirmary, where I had bad flu from a rain-soaked geology field trip around the anthracite fields of Eastern Pennsylvania. My cherished coat is mousy gray muskrat, and although it is not a tough fur, like mink, I feel quite ritzy in it.

Now the mists are burning off Lake Lucerne many miles below. I stretch and yawn and gaze out to my right, through the French doors and over the balcony, to begin a new day with a sight that I am never to see anywhere else, a sight I will keep as my talisman, salting it away forever in a cerebellar back room behind my eyes.

Across from my bed I am looking at clouds. At eye level! Not up at them or down at them, but over at them. They are just out there, my size, grazing like sheep. They coast and dip, lazily, slowly. They have enough altitude above the lake so far below that they feel secure, they know in their cloudy way that they are well up in the sky where they belong. Imagine. Clouds. This close. And, as if they weren't enough to behold, beyond them the Swiss Air Force is practicing its dancing! Small fast planes dive and climb, dive and climb and swoop. No Navy, no wars these Swiss—but high flyers, cloud dancers.

Now the knock at my door. I regather my coat around me. The politeness, the tray, the exit. I devour everything luscious, look over the newspaper, get dressed. So it starts, another perfect morning, up high.

To get here I flew across the Atlantic in a Constellation, a steady old bus with four propellers. All the way over, stopping at Gander (Newfoundland) and Prestwick (Scotland), I sat in the hindermost passenger seat, nothing aft of me but the toilet. The Angels of Safe Flight, clear thinkers like the Elves of Packing, always convince me that plane-crash survivors owe their good luck to having sat in the tail section, which crashes, if not last, at least a little later than the front section.

Impetus for this trip came from Ann, my best friend since seventh grade. From the day we met, we became inseparable friends, and our comradeship lasted all the way through high school. We were complementary, our teachers said. We challenged and mirrored each other. Every year, we danced duets we had choreographed ourselves in modern dance recitals at school: One year we made up a dance for rain and wore get-ups, painted purple and gold, that we'd stitched up from chamois charged to our mothers at Hecht's; another year we made up a galloping dance to the "Ride of the Valkyrie" and had to dump our horned helmets midway through, as they kept falling sideways. For a trip on a train with my mother, when we were in eighth grade, Ann's grandmother made us matching chintz dresses with puffed sleeves. We looked like little slipcovers.

Ann and I did our Latin homework over the phone for hours. We shared more than one boyfriend and every secret. We vied with each other in French irregular verbs, in English exams. We shared large ambitions of success in the big world, as writers, diplomats, dancers. Then we went to different colleges, and our parallel lives began to diverge.

Ann is now winding up law school first in her class, coediting the law review, and mulling over whether to marry an American skier on the U.S. team at the next Winter Olympics after law school. She has cooked up this ski charter, Boston-Zurich round-trip for $350 apiece, and talked me into coming along for the ride, just for Europe on the cheap. To me her reasoning seems flawless, that, in the face of such a bargain, I would "practically be losing money not to go!" So here I am.

I was glad to get away from home base, where I'm still in my first job after college. I'm at the CIA, widely touted All-Ivy Hunting Ground for Mr. Right the Perfect Husband. I am also, time and time again, somebody's bridesmaid. Noodling down aisles in tulle, in taffeta, in Chantilly lace, in *moiré*, in velvet, in *peau de soie*, and back to tulle.

What is to come?

Refreshed, I will come home from the Rigi. Back to more yards and yards of fine bridesmaid fabrics. Back to the paper mountains on my desk at the CIA. In two years, Ann will be maid of honor in my wedding, and a year after that she will come to the Olympics at Cortina and marry her skier, without me. We shall all—the world and I and people I love—be pounded and churned in a surf of loss in the time ahead. And always I will own this one quick visit alone to the Rigi, breakfasting early in mother-soft gray fur while watching clouds and airplanes, out there on the same level as me, dancing together in the blue air.

A Bridge Freshly Tagged
By Ellen Maidman-Tanner

I don't know why the sight hit me so hard, but it did. I first passed the graffiti from the window of a rickety D.C. taxi and then a few days later, while walking south on Connecticut Avenue. The Taft Bridge has been under construction for a few years now, a job that was supposed to have taken only a year, but like the rickety cab, that's just the way things are in the District. So one half, the southbound side with its new concrete, new asphalt, and new metal guard rail, has been open for a few months. That's the concrete that got "tagged." Tagged is the adjective and verb (I tag, you tag, it got tagged) used to describe the act and result of spray-can graffiti bloom, that ubiquitous urban scrawl that lets you know you're not in Kansas anymore. This time, for me, it was highly personal. My bridge, my 'hood.

Anger and sadness had flooded me in the taxi. I went speechless and rigid. Then I was miserable when I walked beside it, running my hands over the newly variegated surface, checking to see if the paint had raised scars like acid on skin. Why here? Couldn't this nighthawk urban artiste appreciate the beauty of the newly minted materials? Didn't a smooth new surface provide the spray-can-bearing vandal the same respite, a place of visual peace, a promise of renewal? Maybe that was the clue to why this sprayer had struck. A swipe. A slap at those who had felt the grace of something rebuilt, the potential that is brought by repair despite the odds in an aging city like Washington. The translation: "Not so fast, oh complacent one. Change is not as easy as new surfaces and renovation. I am here. I am still here. The one who needs to cry out through vandalism is still here." And to prove it, the vandal indelibly marked the territory.

Ah, the childhood. As a well-raised, "capital L" Liberal, I thought of the potential deprivation of the graffitor, the inherent anger, rage, neglect, and abuse, any and all reasons why someone might steal into the night to mar the new beauty of the bridge.

Yeah, maybe.

The older I get and the harder I work, the smaller that L gets, as I move closer to the "we-all-have-choices" camp on the political spectrum. The childhood rationale-pondering did not last long.

The bottom line here was how upset I got, how suddenly and totally upset. My own urban frustration with the decay, the reduction in services, the neglect rose like nausea, and I didn't even know it was there. If the rogue bridge painter wanted impact, he or she had achieved it. I sure noticed the black and blue squiggles, though I couldn't make out the tag itself. Thoughts of acetone and rags danced through my mind. Maybe I'd creep out at 3 a.m. and reverse the job.

But I didn't and I'm still not planning to do that. I'm just writing this down, to capture my own rage for myself, so that I can wonder at the reaction, so suddenly strong for a person who has been a city dweller all her life. At least I found that I was not yet totally numb and immune to the vandalism and for that new awareness I thank the perpetrator. But in the end, that person still had a choice, and I am angered and saddened by the choice that was made.

Routes of Escape
By Caroline Cottom

We're driving along on one of our endless road trips. The road reels toward us, the streaks of tree shadows spooling under the wheels. I'm tired of watching Daddy scratch at his scalp, tired of staring at the flakes that gather on his shoulders like cigarette ash. Mother has been still for almost an hour, gazing at the woods that are speeding past. I want to talk to her, but she seems in a dreamy state.

Ahead, a bridge stretches up toward the clouds, the sun cascading off its metal beams. I sit forward, anticipating the feeling of flying over water.

Daddy cocks his head in my direction. "Carolyn? Are you awake?"

"Yes, Daddy."

"I have a question for you." He clears his throat. "What should I do if a car crosses into our lane while we're on the bridge?"

"Why would they do *that*?" I glance at Cathy asleep beside me, her soft body leaning into the crevice between the door and the back seat. Her head is tilted against the window, her breath making tiny puffs of steam on the glass.

"Someone might fall asleep at the wheel," he explains, "and drift across the center line."

This is hard to believe, and what kind of choice would we have? To smash into the car or plunge off the bridge?

He pauses before speaking. "It would be better to drive off the bridge."

"Into the water?"

"If a car hit us head on, we'd probably all die."

It's late afternoon and the sun is firing the tops of the trees. The flames lick the surface of the river just coming into view.

"If we drove off the bridge, would we float?"

"For a little while. But then the car would sink to the bottom."

I try to think of a good way out, but I can't, which is probably because I'm 8. If we unrolled the windows before we sank, water would come gushing in and we'd drown. The same thing would happen if we waited till we were underwater. And we couldn't just drift down and wait for someone to find us. Wouldn't we run out of air?

I peer out as we start over the bridge. The metal railing looks like it would keep us safe from falling. Isn't that its purpose?

"I don't know what we should do," I tell him.

"Well, we'd open the windows a crack so the water would come in very slowly as the car is sinking. When we had just a little air left, we'd take a deep breath to fill our lungs, unroll the windows all the way, and push ourselves out through the opening. Then we'd swim to the surface."

This is a scary idea. What if I can't unroll the glass? What if I can't push myself out the window, or swim all the way to the top? What if my breath won't last?

"That way," he continues, "the water wouldn't rush in all at once. If it did, there'd be too much pressure on us and we wouldn't be able to get out."

I picture us floating down through a murky soup, Mother staring straight ahead, Cathy crumpled up beside me, eyes closed, clutching her baby blanket. Suddenly the car bumps the bottom, and they wake up. All at once the four of us try to figure out when to roll down the windows. Cathy and Mother have missed the lesson, so they don't know what to do. And I'm helpless. So is Cathy—she's only 4 years old! How could she get out? We would die there, all of us in a metal coffin. Or maybe Daddy would get out alone.

It is one of many explanations Daddy offers for the routes of escape. He has told Cathy and me what we should do if we're asleep and wake up to a blaze in the hallway or a house full of smoke. What to do if we hear a burglar rifling through drawers in another room. What to do if we're riding down a highway and a car comes straight at us in our lane. He's told us stories of how he's pulled people out of burning wrecks, how he's jumped onto the hood of his car when a semi was bearing down on him, the truck so close that it spat bits of gravel onto the car, pitting the paint; how he has driven into gullies and cotton fields to avoid head-on collisions.

Daddy's survival stories and plans for disaster reinforce my sense of the world as a swamp inhabited by reptiles, all hungry and lying in wait. What choice is there but to swim in those infested waters? You can only hope to remain afloat, vigilant and alert, until something happens, not knowing when your life is about to end.

I wonder if danger lurks everywhere, out of sight and underneath the surface.

*   *   *

How To Escape From a Sinking Car. The survival handbook I'm reading as an adult gives different instructions: Open the window as soon as you hit the water. This allows water to come in and equalize the pressure; then you can open the door. Don't wait till the car is underwater. *Get out as soon as possible,* while the car is still afloat. If you're unable to open the window or break it, you have one final option—a course of last resort—and here is where my father's advice comes in: Wait until the car is almost full of water, take a deep breath, open the door (if you are able), and swim to the surface.

The same handbook gives tips for fending off a shark, escaping from killer bees, and avoiding an attack from an alligator. *Should you find yourself in alligator territory, do not swim or wade in areas they are known to inhabit. Also, don't swim or wade alone. Most importantly, never feed alligators. They become less afraid of humans and are more prone to attack.*

I never met up with alligators, but I wish I'd had these instructions when I was a child. Perhaps I would have found clues for my own disaster planning.

*   *   *

In those years we lived in Illinois, first Geneva and later Carbondale. Daddy lived mostly in motels. He would pack a suitcase on Sunday afternoons, spread out the map to show us where he was working that week, and wave goodbye from the front door. He traveled to Peoria, Springfield, and Kankakee, so I imaged there were lots of businesses in those towns. He would call on housewives or business owners—"prospects," he called them—selling encyclopedias or DeWalt table saws.

Daddy showed us pictures of the saws in a plastic binder. In the slick black-and-white photos, steel machines the size of kitchen tables bore their rotary-toothed wheels like fangs. It was the kind of saw that could cut a girl in two, like in the silent movies where the villain, in black cape and mustache, ties the girl to the conveyor belt that is creeping toward the saw. While the saw ground its teeth, buzzing impatiently, waiting for the kill, we were on edge wondering how she could escape. Just when we thought it was too late, the hero would charge up on his steed, dismount, and rush into the sawmill to untie her before her golden tresses reached the blade and her head was severed.

But these were minor frights compared to what awaited us in "House of Wax," a horror movie that came to our local Carbondale theater.

That Saturday Mother dropped us off as usual, with 50 cents for a ticket and a box of candy. The theater was almost empty, unusual for matinees. Were other mothers reluctant to bring their children? We always sat near the back, Cathy on the aisle and me beside her, in case we wanted to get out on short notice. We were on the alert, yet watched the movies as though strapped in, victims of the celluloid, stuck in our velvet seats.

Although everything about this movie reeks of Paris, Hollywood has set the story in New York. A sculptor has created a wax museum with fine renditions of famous people from French history. *Step inside and see Joan of Arc burning at the stake.* "So lifelike," say the museum visitors, "and so beautiful." The sculptor considers these statues his children.

But there is a terrible fire, and all the statues become puddles of wax. The sculptor lives but is burned beyond recognition and can no longer sculpt. Bitter, he opens another museum that he calls the Chamber of Horrors. His face is disfigured and unnaturally pink—Cathy and I later call him "the pink man"—so he creates a mask of his former face to wear during the daytime.

At night, cloaked in black, he sneaks into the morgue to steal bodies, then carts them to the museum cellar, where he coats them in hot wax and turns them into statues. The morgue does not keep an adequate supply of beautiful bodies, however, so he observes museum guests and chooses his kill. "Each subject must be taken from life," he tells visitors. That lovely blond would make a tantalizing Joan, cross clasped in her soft young hands, brown cloak swinging free from her nubile shoulders, a look of sweet martyrdom on her face. That brunette would be the perfect Marie Antoinette.

He swings via rope into the bedroom of the blond woman and strangles her, the next night visiting the morgue to wrest her corpse from its cold chamber. Because his hands are deformed, he uses the rope for strangling and also to drag bodies from the morgue. Cathy and I squeeze hands in the theater, mesmerized by the details of this story. In real life, the blond actress is named Carolyn; in her role, she is named Cathy. Suddenly, my sister and I are thrust into the story as if it were a retelling of our own little lives.

Toward the end, the sculptor stands on the platform talking to the brunette, whom he has captured alive, her body about to be conveyed under liquid wax. The vat bubbles and boils. His eyes glisten with anticipation of the exquisite statue she will become. "Ah, my precious," says the artist-villain. "Soon you will be my beloved Marie Antoinette."

After seeing the movie, Cathy and I lie in wait for the pink man in the grayness of Carbondale nights. Not one night, or two, or three. For months we re-enact the story. Mother and Daddy sleep in another room, unable to hear if the pink man swings in through our window on a rope and, clasping us to his side, swings back out.

At bedtime, before turning out the overhead light, we poke at clothes and stuffed animals in the closet to make sure he's not there. We check in dresser drawers and under our beds. Cathy slips into bed as I make sure the windows are locked, then pull the shades down with a jerk, trying not to see my reflection staring back at me. I dash around her bed to my own and jump in, pulling the chenille bedspread up around my chin. I never cover my head completely, so I'll be sure to see him if he comes. I never lie on my stomach, so he can't surprise me from behind. Are we safe? Has the man lurking outside the window seen me? Is he too lying in wait? Mother and Daddy never know of this scenario that takes place night after night.

Too scared to sleep, we lie so still that anyone would think we are asleep, or, better yet, dead. Try to sleep like this: frozen in place, unable to move because he'll know you're alive, unable to turn over for fear of exposing your back. Even the daisies on the wallpaper seemed to march aggressively those nights. Turn one way, the closet; turn the other, the window and its flimsy yellowing shade with dark creeping in around the edges.

I sleep like this from the age of 12 until I go away to college, never exposing my back in my own house while I lie in bed to sleep.

When I see the movie as an adult, I am surprised to discover that the pink man is Vincent Price. Someone now familiar to me terrified me as a child.

I think about my father, who loved to paint and play the violin. Both he and the sculptor were artists, both addicted to the physical beauty of young females. Was there a pink man inside my father—disfigured, hateful, conniving? Once, when I was 13, I walked in on him as he emerged from the shower. I was shocked at how his penis hung there, flaccid, wrinkled, and pink. I realize now that prior to this incident I had probably only seen it in its erect state.

*   *   *

As soon as Cathy and I begin to share a bedroom, which happens in Carbondale, Daddy stops visiting me at night. I'm in sixth grade, Cathy in second. For the first time she and I close our bedroom door, cover ourselves tightly, sleep as though we are pupas in cocoons, knowing he will not disturb us.

One night a dam breaks, unleashing slabs of concrete and tons of water, which crash down upon me. I awake screaming, which wakes Cathy. I am sure that a horrid death is imminent. Why else would I dream such a terrible thing? I live in a state of fright for days.

Later I think that the dammed-up emotions of enduring Daddy's visits in Geneva and not being able to speak about them had gathered into a mammoth cistern of grief—and now, free of his advances, I could allow the walls to collapse. Or perhaps the safety of Cathy lying near me, able to hear my screams, allowed me to cry out.

Looking back, I wonder if this nightmare followed an incident with Daddy in the kitchen: I am in a white cotton print dress with turquoise, pink, and black bicycles splashed all about. Mother has made dresses of this cloth for Cathy, herself, and me. I'm wearing black flats, a black piqué bolero, black-rimmed glasses. This is the thinnest I will ever be in my life—5 feet, 6 inches and 110 pounds, at the end of an upward growing spurt. I'm on the precipice of adolescence, and life is serious. The refrigerator door is open, as I am taking orange juice out to pour myself a glass.

Enter Daddy in charcoal shirt and slacks, his black eyes particularly sharp. He has something on his mind, and I want to get out of the way, but the refrigerator door is open and my hands are full.

What he says to me—the accusation he hurls—I cannot remember, hard as I try. Is he angry because I'm getting myself something to drink? Have I told Mother something about him that I shouldn't? Have I confided to Mother about the nude man who stands in his doorway when Cathy and I ride our bikes to school? I don't know who has upset Daddy or why it involves me, but I am in his way, and I want to escape.

He jerks the glass and container of juice away from me, sloshing the juice over the cabinet and my freshly pressed dress. Where is Mother? Is she in the house?

"I didn't know you wanted some juice," I say, shaking.

He grabs me by the neck and throws me up against the refrigerator.

I am afraid for my life, unsure what he will do with his violent hands.

In that moment, his right hand slips away from my neck—his left holds my shoulder flat against the cold metal door—and lifts my dress. The eyes are no longer his.

"Daddy! Don't!" I cry out, calling for him as though he is in the next room and can save me.

He glares at me for a moment, then snaps to and drops my dress. He loosens his grip, releasing my shoulder. Then he turns and walks out.

I don't remember what happens next. I probably weep at the sight of my ruined dress, the orange splotches that I must clean up. Trembling, I would wet a dish cloth, dab at the dress and bolero, dab at the cabinet, the floor—and leave the dirty cloth in the sink. I would be afraid to leave the kitchen, afraid for anyone to see me.

But he has left the house. The car starts up in the driveway, the wheels crunch on the gravel and squeal as they hit the street. He has made his escape.

Perhaps the dam collapses after this.

*   *   *

Are my father's attempts to protect Cathy and me from danger actually attempts to protect us from what lurks inside him? Does he know that hunting me like an animal will mark me as prey?

Alligators, like many predators, smell fear in those who might become their dinner. The hunted one emits a scent or signal not unlike a radio transmission.

The fear I carry eventually draws others like my father to me. At age 14, shortly after our family moves to California, I get my first job behind the candy counter at the local theater. Mother, not wishing to drive me to work, loans me her car, even though I don't have a license. I drive to the theater several evenings a week. During this time, Marines from Camp Pendleton follow me down the streets of our town, often stinking drunk. A burly man trails me down the alley behind the theater and tries to force open the door of my car. While I am on retreat with the Girls' Athletic Association, a group of lettermen from my high school confine me in their cabin and start taking off my clothes, intent on rape.

In each instance, something or someone helps me stay coolheaded: I lock the doors of the car instinctively, just in time. I find the closest store or restaurant, so that I am not alone. A Chicano boy from school insists that the other boys stop what they are doing. I never tell my mother about any of this. I am ashamed and feel that somehow each of these incidents is my fault.

During my senior year of college, a student named Gary begins to follow me around campus, dodging behind trees, thinking I won't see him. He is slight, purposeful, walks with dull eyes pointed toward the ground. He never approaches me to talk, but instead writes me letters. In one letter he tells me how much he loves me and asks me to marry him, then lambastes me for treating him so badly, then apologizes for bringing me such grief. On Mother's Day he brings flowers to my dorm, with a note thanking me for being his mom. I go for help to the Dean of Students, whose only suggestion is to keep my distance.

In June I am grateful to graduate and move to Santa Barbara, where my now-divorced mother lives with her new husband. But Gary follows me to Santa Barbara and continues to stalk me. He sends flowers to Cathy, finds out where I work so that he can parade back and forth in front of my office, and knocks on our door at 2 a.m. selling Fuller brushes.

Throughout these incidents, I have no idea that something mutable and distorted in me might be attracting something of like distortion. I assume it is because of how I look (beautiful in a "Natalie Wood," tragic, sort of way, people say), or it is my bad luck. Whatever it is in me, it seems as fixed as a stake driven into the ground. I never think that it has anything to do with my father, because by the time I am 14, I do not remember what he has done.

*   *   *

At 22 I join the Peace Corps, hoping to see another part of the world. I feel compelled to escape to the other side of the planet, unconsciously needing to get as far away from my father and Gary as I can. The Peace Corps obliges, sending me to Thailand to teach English in a boys' secondary school. My two-year tour is pleasant enough, although on several occasions men poke my buttocks under the seats of buses. One day while walking in my town, a man hits me on the breast with his fist. When I report this to the police, they ask, "*Thuk? Thuk?*" Did he hit his mark?

On my trip home through Europe, strange men follow me everywhere. In Vienna someone tries to force open the door to my hotel room late at night. In Athens a man trails me for half a day, until I duck into the stairwell of an apartment building, praying he won't discover my hiding place. A slobbery man with glazed eyes gropes at my body on a Roman bus.

In Florence, desperate for safety, I seek a female companion. An American art student agrees to share her room in a *pension*. The second day I set out for the straw market, a few blocks away. It is a pleasant stroll among old stone buildings layered with history. The market itself, composed of open-air stalls, scatters along two city blocks. I wander for a while before stopping at a stall where the prices are especially low. "Do you have a red wallet like this one?" I ask.

"Not here," says the vendor. "But I have a store nearby, with a much greater selection. Would you like to see?"

I agree and follow him half a block and around the corner. He stops in front of a building with boarded-up windows, descends several steps to a basement, then takes out a key to unlock the door.

"Did you say this is a store?" I ask.

"Yes." He nods, opening the door wide and turning on the light to show me the tables of leather goods. "Actually, a store*house*."

I am skeptical about entering this room that has been locked, where there appears to be no one, but I decide not to act alarmed. I will browse quickly, select a wallet, and leave.

When I enter the room, he closes the door behind me. We are in a musty warehouse with no windows, lit overhead by two bare bulbs. Clearly, I should not be here, but I sense that I must pretend there is nothing unusual about this.

I examine the stacks of wallets, opening them and touching the soft leather. "Oh, here's a red one. Exactly what I'm looking for. How much is it?"

He comes closer to look. "Thirteen hundred lira."

I calculate in my head: it's just a few dollars. "I'll take it." I open my purse and fish around for loose bills.

When I glance up, the man has a narrow leather belt in his hands, which he is twisting around both fists. Very slowly he moves toward me. I continue to dig for the money, moving backward until my back is against the door.

"These are wonderful goods," I say. "Have you had this store long?"

He shakes his head slightly and raises the belt so it is just inches in front of my neck.

I smile. "My mother will love this wallet. She's been asking me to bring her something from Florence."

He stares at me and says nothing.

I glance at the nearest table, then again at him—as though my back is not against the door, as though we are not alone, as though he does not hold a belt to my throat. "Would you mind if I look for something for my sister as well?"

He stares at me for a few more moments, then slowly lowers the belt and gestures toward the merchandise. "Okay. Look." In slow motion, he slips the belt back onto the table.

I select a second wallet, this one brown, and take bills out of my purse to pay him. He makes change from a pouch at his waist.

"Thank you very much," I say and stare as he unlocks the door.

He opens the door, and I start up the steps. I nod and walk determinedly toward the market where dozens of people are gathered at the stalls.

He heads in the direction of his booth as I turn toward the main plaza of Florence, where I hope there will be many tourists. I find a bench in view of the north doors of the Baptistery, stare at the panels of "Agony in the Garden" and "Way to Calvary," and begin to shake.

In the *pension* that night, I continue to shake for hours. I do not speak of the incident to my roommate, with whom I share a double bed, and hope my quivering won't disturb her sleep. Wide awake, I am horror-struck at what I have done, knowing that I might easily be dead.

*   *   *

In Paris I locate a room on the sixth floor of a small hotel, then wander along the Left Bank, perusing artists' paintings of Notre Dame. It is a beautiful city, and I am eager to explore.

Later, in my room, I lie on the thin mattress and gaze up at the window that is hinged outward for fresh air, opening onto Paris rooftops. Suddenly a memory washes over me of a pink man swinging into women's rooms on a rope through casements just like this one. I lie on my back for the next three nights, petrified and watching the window.

*   *   *

I do not tell my mother about my experiences in Thailand, Rome, or Florence. I do not tell her that her daughter is a walking victim, that unbalanced men seek her out, looking to do violence. My mother would have been terrified for me; worse, she would have blamed herself. She is an active alcoholic and reeling from her second divorce. I decide not to weigh her down with what would surely be a startling revelation.

Fifteen years later, at 41, I remember what my father did to me. A string of seven incidents surges to the surface at a counseling workshop after I have witnessed other women recalling their own early experiences of abuse.

I call my mother and tell her what I remember. She says she knew nothing of this. She says that if she had thought my father was harming me, she would have killed him.

I hang up the phone and stare out the window. I recall the early years in Geneva, my bedroom at the top of the stairs, Daddy tucking me in at night. Is it possible she knew nothing? I want to believe that she didn't know, that she would have intervened if she had. But I do not press this question.

*   *   *

I have lived most of my life in the hurricane's path, tossed by waves of sorrow, powerlessness, and despair. I developed chronic muscle pain from holding in terror for so many years, my body weary from stanching the dike. My 17-year marriage could withstand neither my failure to remember nor the flood of recollection.

In time I became willing to investigate the cave that had held me in its hideous grasp—the shifting floor beneath me, the walls covered with ciphers, the ceiling with its incessant drip. As soon as I began to explore, the acts of violence ceased completely. No longer did men approach me intent on harm, not for the next 20 years, not for the rest of my life. I don't know why this is true, but it is. I marvel at the power of simple awareness, the power of bringing secrets into the light.

My father taught me the routes of escape and was also the reason I needed the instruction. He preyed upon me, and because of his preying, I became a victim to others like him. These were the gravest dangers of my life, ones not described in the survival handbook. I have never driven off a bridge, encountered a live alligator, or awakened to a house full of flames, but the principles are the same: When faced with a crisis, keep your head about you, and whenever possible, avoid the swamp.

My father died in 1986. I survived him and all the other predators with my mind, body, and emotions intact. I escaped the perilous waters he had so carefully warned me against.

I continue to explore the cave through writing, counseling, and meditation, and these have made all the difference. Sometimes I encounter my father's dark character drawn on the cave walls, but beside him I see my own glyphs. I trace them over and over in my life as a writer, an act of remembering who I am.

I recall a line from a Sharon Olds poem: "Do what you are going to do, and I will tell about it." This is my recourse, and my path to healing.

Chapter 3

Family Portraits

My Mother's Wings
By Julia Weller

My mother was a cloud writer, looping her winged body into coils of white puffs that wove themselves into words on a sheet of blue, before melting like whipped cream on a summer's day. A stunt pilot before World War II, she flew with the Curtis-Wright Flying Service out of a Michigan airfield. She owned a two-seater biplane and supported herself by skywriting. In photos, my mother is standing beside her plane or leaning from the cockpit. She wears a leather helmet, a long leather double-breasted jacket and jodhpur flying pants, with tall, lace-up boots. She is always smiling.

"What was the happiest day of your life?" I once asked her.

Without hesitation, she answered: "The day I first flew solo."

Ever since she was a child in Sofia, Bulgaria, my mother had dreamed of flying. Her next-door neighbor was a young man named Assen Jordanoff, who left for America to become a test pilot. On his return visits, he held little Olga spellbound with stories of his wonderful flying exploits. She longed to fly too, but he would chuck her under the chin and tease, "Girls don't fly planes!"

That was certainly true in Bulgaria, particularly if the girl was the daughter of the Chief Justice of the Supreme Court. Her father, my grandfather Gencho Handjiev, was a progressive man, who in his youth had studied in St. Petersburg and Paris. He gave Olga and her older sister Vera the same education as their two older brothers and encouraged them to read widely. But when Olga said she

Olga Handjieva, family photo

wanted to fly, he knew his wife would not agree. Paraskieva Matsankieva was interested mainly in beautiful clothes, parties, and her social standing. She would not hear of Olga's embarrassing the family by doing something so tomboyish. It had been bad enough the day "Olya" took one of her skirts, cut it up the middle and sewed it into two trouser legs. When the young girl strode into the drawing room dressed like a man, her mother shrieked: "Oh, my God, what have I done to deserve such a wicked child!" Then she fled to the family chapel to plead with God to help her deal with her difficult burden.

But Olga persisted in being a trial to her. At 17, she heard that the Bulgarian government was offering the winner of a typing contest the opportunity to spend a year at the Bulgarian Embassy in Athens. Olga did not know the first thing about typing, but she wanted to see the world. She bought a typewriter and, in secret, taught herself speed typing from a book. When she won, it was her father who agreed over his wife's objections to let Olga go. She spent a wonderful year in Greece.

Olga's dream of flying had not left her. Her childhood friend Assen sent her one of the books he had written on stunt flying and inside the flyleaf inscribed the teasing words, "To Olya—Bulgaria's first woman pilot?" Back in Sofia, Olga enrolled in the university, studying philosophy. Beautiful, headstrong, and intelligent, she had many admirers. Her friends compared her to Greta Garbo—the same high cheekbones—but her dark brown eyes were larger and her smile was warmer.

One day, Olga came home from classes to find a stranger seated with her oldest brother, Stephan, who imported furs from Canada. The tall, distinguished man bent his sleek black head to brush his lips against the back of her hand. He was a Bulgarian who had emigrated to Canada, where he traveled through the bush buying furs, which he graded and shipped to Bulgaria. The beaver furs were particularly prized for their warmth, softness, and durability. Gabriel G. was 12 years older than Olga, with prematurely graying hair and a lazy smile. Within a few days, he was captivated by her exuberance. He proposed, but Olga just laughed at him. She couldn't imagine marrying someone so old. He pleaded, cajoled, promised to show her the world. Still she rejected him. Then he played his trump card. Stephan had told him of Olga's fascination with airplanes.

"Have you heard of Amelia Earhart?" he asked her one day.

"Of course!" Amelia Earhart was Olga's idol. She waited for him to say what her brother and mother always said, how women shouldn't fly, that it was too dangerous, too difficult, not a woman's place. But he surprised her. "She is not the only one, you know. There are others. If you come with me to Canada, you could learn, too."

Olga thought her heart would stop. Could this possibly be true? Could she really learn to fly? She thought of Assen Jordanoff and all his stories about the new airplanes he had tested and the stunts he had learned. This was what she had always dreamed of doing.

"In that case, yes!"

Olga and Gabriel were married in the Saint Sophia Cathedral in Sofia a month later. Neither her mother nor her brother Stephan was happy about the match.

Both thought she was marrying beneath her social status. Her brother Christo and her sister Vera had reservations for other reasons.

"Will you be happy?" Vera whispered as she kissed her sister goodbye. Olga smiled and murmured softly, "When I am a pilot, I will be very happy."

My mother never talked about her marriage to Gabriel. I learned about her first husband quite by accident, when I needed my parents' marriage certificate and saw, to my surprise, that she was listed as "Widow." It was only after she died that Vera's daughters, who were much older than my sister and me, told us the story of our mother's marriage to Gabriel. There were no children from the marriage and, after a few years, they separated. But Gabriel had kept his promise to Olya. She had learned to fly.

She moved to Michigan and, with another woman, bought a second-hand biplane. She obtained her commercial pilot's license and joined the Curtis-Wright Flying Service. On the weekends, she was a daredevil flyer, performing stunts at air shows and tracing words in the air.

"You know, it looks easy," she said, "but skywriting so that people can read the words is hard. Sometimes the smoke canister would give out in the middle of a letter and I'd have to fire up a new one and then go back and try to fix the half-written letter. But by the time I'd finished, the first letters would already have started to fade."

Airplanes in the early 1930s didn't have complex instrument panels and, in many situations, pilots had to rely on common sense to guide them.

"When you looped the loop, you couldn't tell if you were flying upside down or right side up," my mother once told me. "So I always carried some pencils in my breast pocket. When I got confused, I'd take out a pencil and let it go. If it dropped to the floor, I knew I was right side up. If it flew up past my head, I knew I was upside down!"

Her exploits caught the attention of a wealthy man who decided to sponsor her to be the first woman to fly solo across the Atlantic. Amelia Earhart had already flown across the Atlantic with a co-pilot in 1928, but no woman had yet attempted the crossing alone. In the newspaper

Olga Handjieva, family photo

clipping, the banner reads: "Fair Young Flyer to Try Solo Atlantic Crossing." The paper is yellowed and my mother's portrait photograph is brown with age. Her shoulder is turned so that she is looking back at the camera, a half-smile on her lips, and a curl peeks from under the leather cap. The large goggles are pushed rakishly back on her head. She looks a little wistful.

There is no date on the clipping but my mother told me that only a few months later, it was Amelia Earhart, and not Olga Handjieva, who became the first woman to cross the Atlantic alone. That was in 1932. Her wealthy patron withdrew his sponsorship and my mother never did attempt a transatlantic crossing. After Amelia was lost at sea while on her round-the-world flight with Fred Noonan, my mother decided to sell her plane. It was costly to maintain, and the world's interest in flying had shifted from flight as a form of art to flight as an instrument of destruction.

But before hanging up her wings, Olga returned to Bulgaria and was invited to visit its air force. In the photograph of this ceremony, she wears an elegant fur-trimmed coat with a fashionable hat perched on her dark curls and is surrounded by uniformed officers. Propeller-driven aircraft are parked on the tarmac behind them. In her high heels, my mother is taller than some of the pilots to whom she is speaking and her head is bent forward slightly, as if listening to what they have to say. She is like royalty performing an honor guard review, and they look bedazzled by her presence. I wonder if my mother felt pride at this moment or whether she was secretly laughing at the irony of a woman who had been brought up being told that girls should not fly, now invited to inspect Bulgaria's air force.

Bonding
By Therese Keane

I never thought of my parents as married. They were Mom and Dad—two separate persons who took care of my three sisters and me.

They each had their assigned tasks. Mom did the cooking and cleaning. Dad went out to work every day and fixed stuff around the house. I was so self-absorbed that I saw them only in relation to myself; I never thought about them relating to each other.

Until illness separated them.

Mom checked into a hospital to battle recurrent depression. Dad then had to cook for us and keep us on time for our various activities.

One night after Dad cooked our dinner, I complained about the potatoes or some other vegetables that I declared to be overcooked. Dad sat down, put his head in his hands, and quietly sobbed. His eyes filled up and turned red. "I miss her so much," he said.

I was horrified at his reaction as well as my insensitivity to his attempts at keeping the household intact for us during her Mom's absence.

When I watched them together at the hospital later, I saw the bond that I had never imagined. They were sweetly devoted to each other, holding hands and silently smiling with eyes locked together. They missed each other more than I had realized.

Mom came home after two weeks, and we returned to familiar routines, as though nothing had changed.

But I was changed. I now knew that my parents never took each other for granted. They appeared to work separately for their children, but their invisible bond came into focus for me in a way I have not forgotten.

Portrait of Judge Cook
By Julie Link Haifley

He stares from an ornate gold frame
a quizzical, yet kindly gaze
His formal dress—
midnight waistcoat
crisp white stock
black cravat
and beaver cloak—
portrays a man of means,
judge of others (their crimes unknown)
in western land, young Tennessee.

A painter's strokes on linen cloth
stretched across a wooden frame
as hours lapsed in country inn or tavern plain
tankards clinking, while he limned
the features fine with pigments:
     cobalt, ferrous, zinc
      vivid flesh mid shadows dark.

This handsome face, nose aquiline
with sensuous lips and gentle eyes
soft, brown curls on high and mighty brow
slender jaw, a look benign;
in all, a perfect gentleman.

Sister to Sister (fiction)
By Allyson Denise Walker

I've spent the last several years waiting for The Phone Call—the one from my mother saying, her voice uncertain and shaky with tears, "Oh, Cathryn, I'm so sorry…but your sister is…your sister is…" And although she can't say it, I already know what she's trying to tell me. With a sister like mine, you always expect the worst. At least I did.

Everyone else thought she was the golden girl. With her ready smile, eyes alight with mischief, full of energy and conversation, she charmed everyone she met. Then came the inevitable double take. "There are two of you!" Carolyn would pull me by the arm, saying, "This is my sister. We're twins." She always wanted me with her, like her living shadow, so I was introduced to every acquaintance and dragged on every adventure.

But no one cared that I came along, except Carolyn. I watched and listened, silent and staring, and no one paid any attention to me. I was as taciturn as she was talkative, and I became known as the sullen one.

"Why can't you smile like your sister?" my mother would ask, posing us for the camera in front of the Christmas tree in winter or the backyard swing set in summer. "A smile is so much prettier than a frown." She'd kiss me between the eyebrows, but I could never bring myself to say "cheese." I was more comfortable keeping everything inside and stubbornly tried to accentuate the differences between my sister and me. When we were little and dressed in identical outfits to match our identical faces, people learned to tell us apart by our expressions. Carolyn was always full of enthusiasm and I wasn't.

But then again, I was always taking the blame for whatever Carolyn did wrong. It was her idea to paint pictures on our bedroom wall with magenta nail polish and bake cookies under the broiler to make them brown faster. When she got tired of our mother pressing our hair to a smooth gloss every two weeks, she experimented with a no-lye kiddie relaxer on my head. Naturally, I was the one who was scolded for the second-degree burns on my scalp. If Carolyn spilled or knocked over something when no one was looking, she'd yell, "Cathy!" before I could say anything. I'd learned it was useless to protest, as no one would believe me anyway.

Later, Carolyn learned to slip jewelry, cosmetics, and lingerie in my purse when we shopped. I did her homework while she talked endlessly on the phone. But Carolyn was smart, and what she didn't manage to absorb in class she was able to copy from my test papers.

It became more difficult as the years went by. I couldn't wear the bruised cheek given by an irate boyfriend or match the level of alcohol in her bloodstream and pretend I'd been the one driving. Still, I could claim ownership of the birth control pills she carelessly left on the bathroom counter when we were home on break from college. And I could pay for the abortion she needed when she forgot to take them. If she partied too much the night before a test, she could always score some speed to give her the energy to squeeze in enough studying to pass her classes.

When we rented the inevitable apartment after graduation, I found it more difficult still to keep up the charade. I was the one who called her boss at least once a week—"Carolyn isn't feeling well this morning"—when she was coming down a little too hard to make it in to the office.

When I finally decided to give up being her personal safety net and moved out, Carolyn fell apart. She went from one man to the next, each more abusive that the last, but always rich enough to keep her looking and partying like a star. Sometimes we didn't hear from her for weeks and didn't even know where she was, but she always turned up when she was between boyfriends and needed money.

So I waited for The Phone Call: They'd find her body on the bathroom floor, an accidental drug overdose. Or she'd be shot by a jealous boyfriend or eviscerated by a serial killer she'd picked up in a bar.

I let my guard down when Carolyn got engaged in the middle of her second pregnancy. Johnny had an honest job, as a halfback for the Eagles no less, and she seemed oddly calmed by the changes in her life.

Katherine's Face

Katherine's face is a study. Spring
moves into it and resides there. Her eyes
become variegated marbles,
shining with flecks of green and amber;
her eyebrows arch, each like a new moon
on the verge of dawn.

Her skin takes on the glow
of a nearly ripe peach; for a jaw
she has the graceful contour of
a catalpa leaf; her broad forehead
is a private beach
washed clean by the tide,
presenting a flawless expanse of sand
on which her thoughts may dance.

Botticelli's Venus
rising from the sea on a shell,
she gives us intimations
of divine and earthly love,
at once ethereal and sensuous.
And she will not stain her lips
until the solstice comes.

—Julie Link Haifley

So when I got The Phone Call at 1:00 in the morning in the middle of a snow-storm, the news smacked me in the stomach full force. Johnny and Carolyn had been driving home after a late party and the car had spun out on I-95. Carolyn was in intensive care, and the baby was being delivered two weeks early. Johnny was dead.

*   *   *

Before The Phone Call, I'd had a life of my own. It was a fragile existence at first, carefully put together after I'd abdicated my role as my sister's protector and moved into the tiny efficiency that was all I could afford. I was achingly lonely without the swirl of parties and double dates that revolved around Carolyn. I hadn't realized how much I relied on her for friends and fun or how much I'd miss our private jokes and shared confidences.

Still, I got up every morning and faced the world on my own. I did the sort of work one does with a liberal arts degree in English—writing press releases, handling media contacts, and editing the magazine for a small nonprofit organization dedicated to advancing women's health issues. It didn't pay much, but I found it more rewarding than working in the corporate world. Eventually I made a few friends of my own, and sometimes we stayed up late on weekends hanging out at a low-key bar or drinking coffee in someone's apartment. We'd talk about how we were going to change the world when we had the chance, if we weren't hashing over our relationships with men.

My friends encouraged me to start my own freelance print media business out of my apartment when I got tired of working for someone else. I'd get the shakes over the idea of leaving the security of a steady paycheck, and they'd push me to do what I wanted. But it was Simon who discovered my secret dream, the one I was embarrassed to tell anyone else about.

When I met Simon, he was performing with a Celtic folk group. A couple of friends had dragged me along to see "The River Men" one evening when I had nothing else to do. I was raised on Aretha Franklin, Stevie Wonder, and the Jackson 5. My knowledge of music was built on the stack of 45s that used to sit next to my parents' stereo. I sat mesmerized by this black-haired man with the clear baritone who sang, in a language I'd never heard, melodies that seemed to come straight out of prehistoric Britain.

After the first set, he walked over to me and held out his hand. "I haven't been able to take my eyes off you since you came in and thought I'd introduce myself in order to get to know you. My name is Simon Owens." When we shook hands, he held onto mine with both of his and gave it a gentle squeeze. "Stay and talk to me. I've a few minutes before the next set."

So I did. I had never known anyone who could say and do absolutely anything he pleased without hurting anyone. He told me early on he was a Welsh sheep farmer's son, and I imagined him to be a carefree wandering minstrel who'd just happened to settle on a foreign shore. I later learned that he had a degree in guitar from the Peabody Conservatory and was sought after as a music teacher. Simon didn't have what my parents considered to be a real job, but he seemed content with teaching music and performing with the River Men, whom he also managed.

He was fascinated by my secret dream of writing and illustrating short stories for teens in the style of children's books and comic books. As proud as I was of my small business, I felt incomplete without my writing. My output was copious, but I lacked the courage to get the stories published.

It was Simon who pushed me in his gentle way to places I didn't want to go, to find markets for my work. I had poured all of my courage and creativity into facing the financial risks of running my own business, and here he was asking me to expose my private treasures to public view. I didn't know which was worse, the endless string of rejections or the vulnerability of being in print. I envied Simon's ability to breathe life into his dreams and live them on his own terms, and I told him so. He simply handed me a worn, folded piece of paper with the Prayer of St. Francis—"Lord, make me an instrument of your peace"—written in his left-handed scrawl. He said, "It's my talisman; now it's yours."

Slowly I absorbed Simon's confidence in me and his appreciation of the differences between us. Eventually we moved in together and just when we'd started talking about marriage, Carolyn and Johnny announced their engagement. We couldn't compete with the media attention this news created, so we married quietly with just family in attendance.

Finally I was living the life I was meant for. I was running Pen and Press out of our second bedroom and papering the walls with the rejections that meant I was taking my writing seriously. I never thought it was noble work, but I did a lot of projects for my old employer and had a few other "good cause" clients to balance the boring, corporate ones. I didn't think of myself as living with purpose, but I did begin to have the sense of being guided by a benevolent force in the universe. The Phone Call shattered my serenity, and I had no idea how I was going to pick up the pieces.

*   *   *

By the time the storm let up enough for Simon and me to meet my parents at the hospital, the baby was ready to go home. She was healthy, over 5 pounds, and 36 hours old. She hadn't been named. My parents just stared like blank-eyed puppets.

We were unprepared for the swarm of reporters, photographers, and television crews that materialized as the news hit. The hospital spokeswoman was frantic until reinforcements from the Eagles franchise arrived. I sneaked into the hospital gift shop to buy a pair of sunglasses and ended up giving them to Johnny's mother. She was leaning on her four-pronged cane, her gray head bent, and she looked as though she needed them more than I did.

I was still reeling from the sight of Carolyn lying in the hospital bed, horribly bruised and plugged into a variety of beeping, swishing machines. It was like looking into a macabre mirror that showed what might have happened to me in a parallel universe. I already knew what I'd look like if I wore a clingy red minidress or colored my hair a streaked honey blonde. Now I knew what I'd look like if I'd been found almost nine months pregnant at the bottom of a five-car pileup during a blizzard.

The nurses kept asking us who planned to take the baby. My father broke down and cried the first time he held her, knowing my mother could barely tear herself away from Carolyn's bedside to visit the nursery. Johnny had only one unmarried brother who seemed to be on the 10-year degree plan at Temple University. His mother sat next to me on the waiting room sofa and showed me how to cradle a baby in my arms or snuggle it up to my shoulder.

"You take her home with you," she said. "I'm too old for babies, and your parents have their own daughter to look after."

I knew little about newborns, so I spent most of my time at the hospital learning how to feed and change the baby. I was terrified that this tiny child was to be given over to my inexperienced hands, but it was easier than sitting with Carolyn. After my brief course in infant care, I put Baby Girl Carter in the hospital-issue car seat and took her home, leaving my parents by my sister's bedside.

I worked at home at any hour of the day or night, which turned out to be perfect for taking care of a newborn. The only problem was I got practically no sleep, and when the rare opportunity presented itself I was too consumed with worry and guilt about Carolyn to give in. The doctors said she had little chance of regaining consciousness. Although she was breathing on her own again, the head trauma had been too severe, and she was still bleeding internally. During those rare times when I wasn't dealing with deadlines or dirty diapers, I went to the hospital.

"Get some rest, you look like a mess," my mother would say, watching me worriedly with dark-circled, puffy eyes.

"Yeah, yeah, right back atcha," I'd respond and give her a hug.

*   *   *

Simon suggested a name for the baby—Keridwen, Keri for short. Keridwen is his mother's name and it sounds sort of like Carolyn—a good combination. I was still overwhelmed by the enormity of it all. I'd no idea that babies were so exhausting. I'd no idea that grief and worry were so exhausting. I lay awake at night, questioning God on my fate and Carolyn's. Why was I given this child to care for while my sister lay dying in the hospital? I didn't want to spend my nights walking the floor with a screaming infant and my days preparing formula and packing the diaper bag for the grand odyssey of leaving home with a baby. I wanted my old carefree existence and I wanted my twin sister back. Carolyn had been on the brink of pulling herself together, of starting a new life, and now it had been ruthlessly snatched from her. And no matter how hard I tried to run away from it, I always seemed to end up shouldering her responsibilities as well as my own.

Despite my resistance, Keri awakened a fierce protectiveness in me. She was so small and vulnerable, and I found an unexpected peace in her contentment. Then my breasts began to swell and ache excruciatingly. Simon took us to the hospital on a double mission—to visit my sister and find out why my breasts felt like twin hand grenades ready to explode at any moment. The nurse assured me that everything was fine. It didn't happen often, she told me, but sometimes adoptive mothers can start lactating. I was amazed. My breasts were preparing to feed the child that my arms had been caring for these past weeks.

*   *   *

My milk came in on the day my sister died. When I went to see her that last day, she was fighting to breathe; the effort of it seemed to be enough to wake her. Still, she lay as though asleep but not at all peaceful.

The doctors wanted to put her back on a ventilator but they offered no hope of recovery. My parents and I had a grim meeting in the waiting room. "Sticking a tube down Carolyn's throat again to inflate and deflate her lungs would be cruel at this point," my mother said. "If she's going to recover, she'll have to do it without the ventilator."

I went back to her room and took the hand that didn't have any needles and tubes running out of it. I pleaded with her to wake up and get better, offering up prayers for a miracle. She took one rattling breath, then waited. I squeezed her hand and called her name, panic rising within me. She took another sighing breath, and I exhaled in relief. But that was all. The sporadic beeping of the monitor ran together into one long whine. Or was it the sound of my screams?

The nurses came running and pulled me away from Carolyn as I tried to cling to her, begging her not to leave me. They led me from the room and herded me down to the waiting room where Simon and my parents were sitting with Keri.

I was still screaming and sobbing, eyes and nose streaming. A nurse held a cool cloth to my face while one of the doctors suggested giving me a sedative. I couldn't; it might get into Keri's milk.

It was Simon who calmed me. He handed Keri to me and wrapped his arms around both of us, murmuring comforts in Welsh. Then I felt something warm and wet soaking my top. Simon sat me down and held me close while I tried to put Keri to my breast. She was all I had left of my sister.

*　　　　　*　　　　　*

So I sit in my rocking chair in the dawn twilight, the only time I have to myself, thinking about the hand I've been dealt and wondering whether I have the strength to play it. I'm still trying to figure out how I ended up with my dead sister's child when I am a storyteller, not a mother.

It goes against the code of womanhood, but I'm not fond of babies. They are noisy, messy, demanding, and exhausting, and you never know what they're thinking. Everyone says they admire me for what I'm doing, like it's some selfless, noble act; but inside I'm selfish and rebellious. I keep thinking, *I don't want this— I don't want this.* Then I think about the way Keri studies my face during her wakeful moments and cuddles while nursing, and I realize I'm watching my thoughts chase themselves in circles.

Simon asked me last night, "So why are we doing this?"

"Because we have to," I replied automatically.

"Don't we have a choice?" he asked.

I looked down at Keri in her borrowed bassinet. "No. We don't have a choice." I walked over to the window and looked out at the bare branches of the trees against the darkening late winter sky, their buds barely visible. "If there's any choice here, it seems to have chosen us."

He reached over and tucked a curl behind my ear. "I chose you. From the first moment I saw you I knew you were meant for me. But you had to choose me as well. It's the same here. We're doing this because we want to."

"But I don't *want* to!" I cried out. I took a deep breath and turned back to the window, away from his probing eyes. "I don't want this responsibility," I whispered.

"Then what do you want?"

This stopped me. I hadn't considered what I wanted, only what I didn't want. I said slowly, "I want to write my stories and run my business. And I want my sister back." My voice cracked then, but I cleared my throat and blinked to keep the tears away.

"And what do you want for Keri?"

"I want for her to grow up strong and smart and beautiful."

"Like you," he said, with a smile like a caress.

I bit my lip and a tear ran down my cheek.

I thought I had found my purpose in life. I thought I had discovered the frightening truth that following one's divine path might not lead to comfort but always leads to joy. Only now I have a little one to lead down the path as far as I can take her. And I remember the old bedside prayer that Johnny's mother quoted to me when I took Keri home from the hospital, "The will of God can never lead you where the grace of God cannot keep you."

Behind Julia's Eyes
By Barbara Shine

By the time I joined Bob's life and met his mother, her cognitive powers were fading. But her appearance was flawless. Julia at 83 had white hair in wispy waves; a trim, upright, size-10 figure; and eyes of the loveliest soft blue.

At our first meeting, in Akron about 7 years ago, Julia displayed the grace, carriage, and manners of a Southern aristocrat, and her voice emerged in a charming Carolina drawl. It's not the thick Karo accent of caricature; her voice is just softly inflected, as subtly appealing as honeysuckle nectar. Julia likes to tell the story about how, after moving to Ohio with Bob's father, she took classes to erase her accent. And the punch line?

"The speech teacher said I couldn't *possibly* be helped, so he refunded my tuition." Sometimes she tells this story five times in an hour.

When Julia tells stories, her bright eyes offer me a glimpse of the woman she used to be, before Alzheimer's disease became her own.

In old pictures, I've seen Julia in her fitted Wanamaker suits and afternoon hats, a defiant white streak of hair tearing upward from a broad forehead to disappear under a tiny veil. Posed with her garden club friends or other executives' wives, she faces the camera not quite head-on, with finishing-school posture and a slightly tight smile admitting a strained tolerance for the photographic obligation.

The woman in those old black-and-white photos—the young mother, suburban clubwoman, well-to-do matron—had eyes as cool and composed as Arctic ice. They were crystalline windows on her well-ordered world. Julia's clear gaze was that of a self-possessed woman: She knew her position and her possibilities; she knew where she was going.

Today, 40 or 50 years later, Julia usually doesn't even know where she is. A few summers ago, we brought her to Maryland to be near us. She lives in Applewood, the dementia nursing unit at the health care center we chose for her. The euphemism "health care center" has been a blessing: It means we don't have to tell Julia she's in a nursing home. Her faltering memory is tricky, but she *does* remember that "nursing home" means something she wants to avoid.

The first time I saw Julia in her room at Applewood, those lovely eyes were clouded by pain and bewilderment. She could neither comprehend nor accept the strangeness around her. Julia is perpetually confused, but she's not oblivious to her surroundings. She could see that some of the other Applewood residents acted strangely, and they frightened her.

Julia moves in and out of that anguishing stage where she is aware that her mind is changing and terrified by her inability to control it. "Am I goin' crazy?" she asks. And we can offer her only calming drugs and platitudes.

Over the years, the bright assuredness in Julia's eyes has diminished as her memory and acuity, even her universe, have shrunk. In moments of doubt or worry, her eyes are the careworn blue of a denim shirt loved nearly to exhaustion.

After a year or so in Applewood, Julia would less often ask to go home; she does not truly remember where "home" is. Sometimes, blessedly, she thinks Applewood is home, that it belongs to her; but then she treats the other residents as rude, stubborn, badly dressed houseguests. The handsome brick-front house in Akron, where she raised Bob and survived three husbands, is gone from her memory, as are the last two husbands. Bob's father she can sometimes recall if we prompt her with old pictures from their Hawaiian cruise or summers in Arizona.

Her deeply ingrained Southern manners have served Julia well as more recent memories fade. When we visit the nursing home, Julia might take Bob's arm and discreetly inquire, "Now, what name shall I use when I introduce you to people?" Bob cheerfully supports the charade when he answers, "Oh, we don't need to be formal: Just say, 'This is my son Bob.'"

At each visit, Julia introduces us to one special friend, Mrs. Borden—after asking the lady's name, of course—and the friend smiles brightly every time. I don't know how we'll handle it when Mrs. Borden forgets her own name and can no longer assist in this ritual of courtesy. But we'll figure something out: The family playing host to Alzheimer's disease is rich in opportunities for problem-solving.

*   *   *

From the beginning, Julia seemed delighted to know me, gracious and welcoming in every way. Yet this lovely woman had, every few days for months, thrown all of her husband's clothes into the garage, screeching that he must move out. And she repeatedly locked her home health aides in the basement, suspecting they were out to steal that same husband. When Bob and I were not there, she told visitors her son was plotting to get her money.

During our early visits to Julia's home, before the nursing home became a must, when she would leave the living room briefly (she went off to change clothes every hour or so), she was clearly surprised on returning to find company in her easy chairs. But her innate gentility carried the day. With just the barest flicker of an eye, and without skipping a beat, she'd offer some transitional comment—"Isn't this weather delightful!"—and then say to me, "I'm sure we've met, but I'm afraid I've forgotten your name."

I used to think about giving funny answers after the second or third reintroduction—calling myself Esmeralda or Priscilla and saying I was there to give tap dance lessons, but I resisted that wicked urge. Eventually, to reduce my frustration and ward off any impatience with Julia, I looked for and found an attitude adjustment. I suddenly realized that, with this woman, as with no one else in my life, I have virtually *endless* opportunities to make a *good first impression*. And so I shall. Julia may not remember me from one visit to the next, but I'll try to make sure that she likes me every time.

*　　　*　　　*

Since moving to Maryland, Julia has lost much of her soft white hair, and she continually apologizes for her appearance. I always respond, "You look real pretty today, though."

Then she answers with great cheer: "Oh, I used to be pretty. I was Miss America, you know." The young and beautiful Julia Stanley was, in fact, awarded some sort of title at her state teacher's college, but in the memory behind Julia's eyes, that title translates to "Miss America."

I answer with amazement: "Really! When were you Miss America?"

"What year was it, J.T.?" she asks Bob, who for the moment she sees as her older brother.

"I'm not sure," he says, "but you must have been in your 20s."

"How old am I now?" she asks.

"Why, you're 113," he answers, winning much-needed laughter from both wife and mother.

"Well, I'm not very pretty anymore," Julia confides to me when the laughter subsides, "but the men still like me, they still flirt! I was Miss America, you know."

And that's my cue for another guilt-free lie: I tell Julia, "You are as beautiful as ever."

She squeezes my hand and seems content with my answer. Bob takes in this tableau and beams at both of us—the wife he's recently found and the mother he's slowly losing.

Julia may not believe all my lies, but at least she has faith in my good intentions. Or maybe she just approves of my nice manners. Anyway, I see trust behind Julia's glimmering eyes.

For My Daughter, With a Gift of Blue Butterflies for Her Ears
By Nancy Galbraith

To Alexandra

Family photo

Butterflies are delicate we say
But look! They struggle open
great with effort.
One burst of muscle
rips wings free
leaving empty to the air
their tight warm sticky rags.

Is it so sad?
My love, it is like being born.
Out of the warm
to come alive.

You and I
went through it once.
Today, again.
Now yet again, you're 46.

Being born then
   you had to say
and mean it with your brave body
   "I must be out of here."
   We lived on one heartbeat first,
   then two, talking
blood secrets
   in our sweet dark sleep.

   Came the time
to shove each other hard
   we pushed away
with all our muscle.
   We push apart today
   though I would hold close yet
   as then, around you.

Butterfly and psyche,
one strength does for us both
   only at our beginning.
   Strong winged, more fair than I
   you fought me fair.
   Your strength is yours
   and not come easy.
   Fly free.

Chapter 4

Friends and Other Animals

Coffee Break
By Lori Carruthers

A freshly brewed cup of coffee sipped at a coffeehouse is a rediscovered pleasure of mine. I don't go out every day for coffee like many of my co-workers, who make a daily trek with refillable plastic mugs, to the express storefront across the street. A gigante café au lait in a ceramic cup is what I linger over at the coffeehouse near my downtown Washington, D.C., office.

It may be the rich flavor of the coffee that takes me back in time, nearly two decades, to Seattle and the Grand Illusion. Named after a French film, it was part coffeehouse and part cinema and my refuge. It was cool without trying to be, long before coffeehouses had mass-market appeal. Located in the University District, we regulars were young but not exclusively students. The Grand Illusion was home to those who could find entertainment and comfort in a fresh cup of coffee.

The seating area held just a few tables ringing the room. White linen cloths topped the small square tables that were protected by a practical slab of thick, clear glass. In cooler months, which could be anytime in Seattle, the coveted seat was the maroon horsehair sofa facing the fireplace. Prints of nymphs and water-falls by Maxfield Parrish graced the walls and added to the aura of artistic non-chalance.

Café au lait was served in standard-issue, white, restaurant coffee cups with gray scratches on the inside, etched by the stirring of spoons. Regular coffees came with free refills, but I cannot remember ever ordering a plain cup of coffee, despite its bargain price.

Sometimes I went to the Grand Illusion alone, but most of the time I met Kay or Anna or Jane. Anna was my friend and confidante from undergraduate days. Jane and Kay were her housemates and our friends. Being underemployed, we four had the time to nurse our café au lait for hours. We read and discussed books, the characters becoming our new friends. Religion and politics were never taboo subjects but provided opportunities to see and understand another's point of view. We supported one another in our choices, even if not always agreeing with the decision reached.

We four were all quite different. Kay was older than the rest of us and joined the military months before her 35th birthday. Now, 20 years later, she is the only one of the three with whom I still correspond. She challenges me with her ideas and supports me with her words. Jane was the youngest and the artist of the group. She crafted Venus figures in felted wool, exploring feminine shapes as she formed her sexual identity. I regret that the thread of communication with Jane unraveled and I never got to know the woman that she grew into being. Anna, my bright college friend, sought her identity in the arms of an abusive soldier. Our friendship dissolved as the time she spent with her lover overshadowed her time with us.

Now, my jaunts to the café are with a newfound friend and colleague. She and I discreetly schedule our coffee rendezvous when we've had a bit too much of the office politics or, more rarely, we have some news to celebrate. One of us covertly sends an e-mail to the other to schedule and confirm the outing; then we slip away from our desks and meet at the elevator.

Karen and I talk about our husbands and our aging parents. Work often invades our conversation, but we still have the time and interest to linger over ideas. We lend support to one another but are wise enough to forgo unrequested advice.

So now I sip cappuccino on the other side of the country from where I started, slouching comfortably in a modern upholstered chair. Granulated sugar is dusted over the milk foam covering the dark rich espresso mixed with steamed milk hidden below. I share these sweet moments with a newfound friend and remember the old, happy to have the time and companionship to once again savor my cup of coffee.

Turtle Waltz
By Julia Weller

I was driving to work along a winding road bordering the old C&O Canal in Washington, D.C., enjoying the serenity of sunlight sparkling between green leaves, when I rounded a bend and saw up ahead a large turtle standing immobile on the gravel shoulder. It was the size of a washbasin and the color of sweat-soaked leather. Its head projected stiffly toward the road, only inches from the passing cars. One foot was raised over the asphalt, frozen in position, as if awaiting the signal to cross. I slowed down but the turtle made no move.

Surely it wouldn't be so stupid as to try to cross the road? I wondered. Should I stop and try to move it off the road? If I did I would be late for work.

I drove past, still arguing with myself, and looked back in my rearview mirror. The cars behind me were swerving slightly to give the turtle more room in case it suddenly decided to step out. But its foot was still poised majestically in midair.

I braked sharply and pulled over onto the shoulder, then reversed until I was within 10 feet of the turtle. He didn't flinch at the sound of my car approaching, nor did he turn to look at me as I walked toward him, my high heels crunching in the sandy dirt. His down-turned mouth and bald head gave him the sour look of a degenerate old aristocrat. I bent over, arms outstretched to grasp the sides of his shell when he suddenly launched himself upward, his neck twisting 'round and his mouth open. I felt the edge of his jaws brush the skin on the inside of my arm and heard the cracking sound of a trap snapping shut. I leapt back, my arms flailing like a tightrope walker losing her balance. My heart was pounding from fright. I had expected to be the rescuer, not the victim.

For a moment I considered abandoning my attempt at heroism, but the turtle's aerial assault had landed it even closer to the rush-hour traffic. One front leg and one back leg were now on the road, and it was facing away from the oncoming cars. One careless swerve by a preoccupied driver would crush this crusty old reptile. I looked around for a long stick to use as a lever. In the high, papery grass under the branches bowed with kudzu, I saw one. Bending low to keep my hair from getting tangled in the creepers, I stepped in among the undergrowth. My patent leather shoe sank deep into squelching mud. At the same moment, a twig snagged my other leg and I felt the nylon rip. As I stood up to extricate my shoe from the swamp, a branch speared my hair from above.

Uncharitably, I cursed the mud, the turtle, and the Japanese for importing kudzu. I cursed the inventor of high heels. Then I cursed myself for stopping. Finally free, I grabbed the dead branch and emerged from the undergrowth looking a little less poised than when I had entered it. I stomped toward the cursed turtle. Come what may, I was going to rescue the blasted thing. It had not changed position and still chose to ignore me. Standing well back, I slid the stick alongside the turtle, hoping to nudge him off the road. But he was heavy and I realized I would have to apply more pressure. I pushed and for a moment nothing happened. Then as suddenly as before, the turtle shot up, twisted around and grabbed the branch in his mouth. With a jerk he pulled it from my grasp. However, this time when he landed, he was no longer on the road and was now turned toward the kudzu.

That gave me an idea. If I could goad him with a stick, perhaps I could get him to leap toward the grass. Or if he held on to the stick, I could drag him off the shoulder and roll him down the bank into the woods below. But, as with so many of life's little theories, it didn't work in practice. Even though I held on to the stick on my next attempt, the turtle didn't and the next leap left him facing the road again. I gave him another poke and he took another flying arabesque, this time landing sideways.

We seemed to be doing a little dance, the turtle and I, sometimes moving forward, sometimes back. I had a sudden picture of myself, a lady in a gray silk suit and mud-covered pumps, waltzing with a turtle by the side of the road. Out of the corner of my eye, I saw cars slow down as they passed and caught a glimpse of bemused smiles.

Suddenly, a red car rounded the bend on the shoulder and came racing toward us. I straightened up, thinking the driver had not seen me, and waved my arms wildly. The battered Datsun came to a stop in a cloud of brown dust a few feet from where I was standing. A dark-skinned man in heavy-rimmed glasses flung open the door and jumped out.

"Elijah Gabriel, professor of zoology!" he announced as he came running toward me with his hand outstretched. "I was driving in the other direction and I saw you trying to move this creature off the road, so I did a U-turn and came back to help you."

His impetuous greeting left me momentarily speechless. My next instinct was to hug him. Instead I took his hand in both of mine, pumping it up and down furiously.

"Thank you! Thank you so much!" I babbled, "I really didn't know what to do. He's so big and I tried to lift him and...."

I told my story of almost being bitten by the turtle and my surprise at the attack.

"Well, that's why they call them snapping turtles, you know!" the professor said cheerfully and dashed back to his car. My rescuer seemed to be bursting with kinetic energy and his speedy movements left me a little dazed. I followed, feeling rather stupid. Of course! Why hadn't I realized that this was a snapping turtle? I reflected that my knowledge of the animal kingdom was decidedly limited. When

I reached him, the professor was busily rummaging around inside the trunk of his car and emerged at last with a long-handled ice scraper.

"This should do it!" he announced.

With a few swift strokes, he rolled my dance partner away from the road. The professor was slightly built, in his early 30s, and a few inches shorter than I. He wielded the ice scraper with the grace of an orchestra conductor so that the turtle never succeeded in grasping the handle and snapped angrily at the air.

"He probably crossed the road during the night to get to the water and may have been trying to get back to the woods on the other side," the zoologist explained. "But he's safer at the bottom of the hill. This one is very old. It would be a shame to let him be killed."

As he worked, flipping the turtle over and over in the gravel until it looked like a breaded drumstick, the professor and I talked. There was a companionable sense of common purpose that dissolved the barriers that would normally have separated two strangers. He told me that he taught at Howard University and that he was from Ethiopia. He guessed from my accent that I had lived in England and told me he had studied there, too. We compared notes on our English public school experiences.

Wave Walking

As I stroll the cold sand, I listen to the sea. Her waves never lose their rolling energy—sometimes robust, sometimes languid.

I try to hear her whispers inside the lush rumblings of her surf. Her sound slowly fades as each wave hits the shore, flattens out, and lazily floats back into her larger body. She tries to make contact, reciting the same surfing litany, floating over my foot to get my attention.

Today, the wind has given her a headdress of white caps that bob and sink into her thick waves of dark blue hair.

Birds unrelated to each other—large white-feathered gulls, tiny brown sandpipers, and velvet-black crows—share the seashore neighborhood. Their sharp eyes race for the microscopic urchins deposited by the retreating surf. The shorebirds understand what the sea means to them. What does she mean to me?

—Therese Keane

"My housemaster was a very jolly fellow," he said, his language a mixture of British and American, accented in Amharic. "I stayed with him and his wife during the hols because it was too expensive for me to go back and forth to Ethiopia. He tried to convince me to become a member of the Church of England." The professor gave a high-pitched laugh as he recalled the incident, as if he found it a little embarrassing.

Once we reached the undergrowth, heaving the turtle over and over became more difficult because of the tree roots and tangled grass. The professor had to stop more often to push his thick, black-rimmed glasses up the bridge of his nose. He asked me whether I was Church of England, and I told him that I had converted to Judaism because of my husband. He listened intently to my story, sometimes looking straight at me as if to assure me that he was paying attention.

I didn't find his questions intrusive or strange and asked him just as many. There was a complete absence of role-playing or sexual undertone. We talked freely, without fear of judgment. Our joint mission had thrown us together, creating a separate reality and momentarily suspending all social conventions. We were like passengers on an airplane who would never dream of talking to strangers on the bus, telling their seatmates their life stories within minutes of sitting down. Listening to the cadence of my companion's rapid speech as he painted in words the colors of his Ethiopia, I almost forgot why we were there. Rescuing the turtle had become of secondary importance.

At last we reached the edge of the slope.

"This is it, old man!" said the professor, addressing the turtle. One final shove sent the turtle, still snapping angrily, bouncing down the hill through the trees. We stood silently for a moment trying to make out its shape at the bottom and I realized that I didn't know what to say. Without the turtle to bind us together, the spell was broken. We were two strangers once more.

I wasn't sure how to end the encounter. Should I shake Professor Gabriel's hand again? What was the protocol for marking the end of a rescue mission? I hadn't much experience dealing with knights in shining armor.

"Well, thank you again," I mumbled.

"No problem!" The professor darted out of the woods and back to his car. Before I even started the engine of my car, he had done a U-turn and was driving off in the direction from which he had come.

Brunching on the Far End of the Food Chain
By Nancy Galbraith
For Captain Scott O'Grady

Because my current housekeeping skills are lite, because I am moving from one apartment to another, because I am a keeper and not a tosser of junk, and because I do not always rinse out implements that have been washed in recent memory, the journeys of certain specific insects have intersected my life at notable moments, creating this morning's reflections.

A few days ago I made a small thermos of coffee to accompany me on errands in the car. A small thermos with a mouthpiece in its lid. At a stop light I took a sip and felt in my mouth along with the exotic mocha coffee a little, nearly weightless bit of fluff. Thinking it might be a leaf (no logical reason to think this, it just felt like a honeysuckle leaf), I made one of those instant decisions: to not swallow it, even though I am not a finicky eater and have no dietary problems with honeysuckle.

I spat it into my hand as I moved forward on a green light, and what then should lie on my palm but a cockroach. Not a juicy live speedster but its dried-out carapace. "Pfaawgh!" I naturally enough said ("feh" in Yiddish) and went on to have two writerly thoughts:

1. Do a learned essay, "Entomology in Everyday Life: Unappetizing Insects That Have Found Their Way Into My Face and the Faces of Those I Love."
2. Reflect! Learn when to write a poem, when to write an essay, and when to just shut up and kick back with some relaxing little solid geometry problem and maybe a beer.

Now, two other noteworthy oral encounters of the six-to-eight-legged kind are, briefly, these:

A gnat flew into my husband's mouth in a tennis game last summer. So tiny, so fast, it went on down. He ate it. And I, culinarily curious, asked, "How was it?"

"Not bad!" he said. "Tasted kind of like venison."

Second incident. Eating my vegetable salad at the Palace of Culture cafeteria, I bit down on what felt like a dried-out pea. Deciding prophetically to not eat it, I was stunned to find in my hand one-half of a quite crunchy black beetle. Well, you can see how, lacking eye contact with this small being, anybody might mistake it for a dried legume! That a half-bug lay listless across my palm strongly suggested I had eaten the other half. In fact, when I stormed into the kitchen and confronted the cafeteria manager with my little prize, he asked not how I was, but where the rest of the bug was.

Chapter 5

Body and Soul

Living on Planet Drum
By Barbara Shine

Thah-dump. Thah-dump-dump.
  Thah-dumpbumbum.
  Thah-dump-bum-biddybiddybiddybiddybump-badump.
This is my heart, in unseen, muffled, but insistent rebellion. A noisy dys-rhythmic protest against—what? Its unfair workload? The years I abused it? Its anticipated collapse?

I've just rolled over, settling into the best posture for my night's rest. My left arm reaches around Bob's warm, solid middle, and he *mmmm*'s in response. It sounds like his smile, and I smile back, into the dark. In sleep, he reaches for my hand against his chest, and I wriggle closer, spooned against his back.

A few seconds later, my chest speaks, and I'm suddenly wide awake again. This is spell number six or eight for the day, but somehow the daytime attacks don't inspire so much fear. At night, lying next to my new husband, I worry about what all this means for him.

I listen to the flutters interrupted by deep booms, and behind closed eyes I can see the feeling: It's a large fish, gasping and flopping frantically inside a kettle drum. I feel the slap and slam of agitated heart muscle against the chest wall and wait to find out my future.

Thah-dumpdumpdump-biddybiddy-bump. Thah-dump.
I've had these feelings before, and my doctors diagnosed atrial fibrillation, "a-fib" for those in the know. It's less serious than "v-fib"—ventricular fibrillation—which causes sudden death, but it's serious enough. A-fib often triggers deadly or disabling strokes.

I cannot sleep while I wait for my heart to either normalize or burst up through my windpipe. This aberration of rhythm holds my thoughts like the opening hook of a Michael Crichton thriller: Will the beats soon revert to nor-mal? Or will this be the time when the crazy flutters—*biddybiddybiddy-bump-bumpbum*—accelerate to the quiver of exhaustion that precedes a flat EKG? Or maybe worse, will the gyrating heart muscle eject a blood clot, swooshing it through the arteries to my brain?

If the pounding and fluttering don't stop pretty soon (but what's "pretty soon"?), I'll have to go to the emergency room. How long is it safe to wait? Can I decide by myself? Yes, I can. I try not to let this be Bob's problem too.

My heart has always been something of a renegade, racing, slowing, skipping beats. I was born with a mitral valve defect that worsened when I had rheumatic fever in early childhood. I was fully an adult before I understood that not every-one can feel and hear their heartbeats as I do.

In my 20s I invented a crude sort of biofeedback (though I had not yet heard of that technique) that I used to slow my racing heart. When the beats started coming too fast, I'd start singing—just silently, in my head—'Way down upon the Swanee River, far, far away...' I started singing fast, in time to the rapid beats. Then, gradually, I slowed my mental singing and the runaway heart rhythm slowed with it.

Twice my heart has given in to infections and hosted rapacious bacterial colonies, sheltering those enemies and feeding them with the tissue of its very walls and gates. And eight years ago, my fragile heart literally broke—at least the cords that work the mitral valve did: They tore from their moorings and could no longer open and close the valve leaflets.

So the surgeons requisitioned a new mitral valve for me, one fashioned from the generous-sized heart of a pig.

My sons bought me a copy of *Charlotte's Web* to celebrate my porcine acquisition, and over time, my new valve and I adjusted to each other. But the prosthesis carries no special curative powers. My poor old heart (I can see it as almost a separate, ravaged person), worn and weary far beyond my not-yet-50 calendar years, has had to struggle all along. From decades of illness and unwise exertions—I was a drum majorette, loved fast dancing, bore three children, and smoked and drank to excess—my heart is far larger and hence less hardy than it should be. It is inelastic and spongy. It feels crowded in my chest.

One day just over a year ago, my heart started jumping around in those crazy rhythms and, oddly, it didn't stop after its usual few minutes of tom-tomming. It didn't stop all day, and the sound-feelings became deeper, more profound. More rest, I thought; working too hard; get more sleep. I kidded myself that way until, after three or four days of relentless fatigue, I decided that the manic riffs of "Wipeout" bouncing around my sternum, alternating with cannons from the "1812 Overture," might warrant a professional's opinion.

My stoicism brought a tough lesson. I was sternly chided for procrastinating, rapidly admitted to George Washington University Hospital, infused with cardiac drugs and IVs of blood thinners, and closely watched for symptoms of stroke or internal bleeding. By waiting for days, I had greatly increased the risk of a stroke. After we found that the meds alone could not regulate my heart rhythms (and I held little hope for success with "Swanee River"), I was treated to a procedure called cardioversion. The docs put me to sleep just briefly while they applied an electric jolt of several hundred joules to my chest.

I think this real-life take on Rescue 911 ("Clear!") was supposed to scare my heart into behaving properly, but it didn't work the first couple of times. Hey, this is not a faint-hearted heart! Eventually, though, the shamans of the ampere prevailed, and my rebel heart settled into a fairly normal pace and rhythm.

I left GW Hospital with painful burns on my chest, a tube of Thermazene to assuage them, and prescriptions for a heart medicine that could be more deadly than the condition we're treating and an anticoagulant that is basically the stuff that's used to kill rats by causing internal hemorrhages. Between the drug side effects and the electric shock episode, I also carried home a residue of anxiety and depression that took months to subside.

Then, about six months ago, it happened again. As I sat working at my PC: *Thah-dump. Thah-dumpdump.* Then a few more, then back to normal. I took a few deep stress-management-seminar breaths, ambled into the kitchen for a soothing cup of tea, and decided there was really nothing wrong.

But now it happens more and more often, every day and every night, and I am both scared and curious. I'm frightened about pain and the prospect of disabling illness, but unlike most people, I don't dread a hospital stay. I am a good patient (I've had lots of practice), and my fascination with medical procedures prevails even while I'm at their center.

Thah-dumpbumpbump. Thah-dump-bumbiddy-bumbiddybiddy...

What if my heart takes off on a flight of unremitting tympanic abandon, what will happen next? Recently I heard about a promising new treatment for a-fib that lets the docs go in with a catheter and actually administer little electric burns *right inside* the heart! Wow, what an advance: Let's bypass those pesky skin burns and go for some *real* damage! This procedure is terrifying to ponder; I'm certainly not ready to try it.

Today I have an electronic companion nestled close to my heart. Like a baby in one of those canvas

---

Forced Watch

Mom's fingers have forgotten the piano keys; her feet no longer love a polka beat. She writes invisible lists with a fork and eats string beans with her hands. When she sniffles I hand over a tissue, which she folds into quarters and tucks under a sleeve while her nose drips unchecked. Mom seldom complains, but neither does she sing. Her pale blue eyes, faded from the deep, piercing, chocolate brown of young motherhood, seem free of worry, but they are likewise devoid of joy.

I'm helpless while a sculptor I cannot see or dissuade chisels away the sharp corners and tender bulges that made my mother unique. Her features and personality, even her voice, tend toward the smooth sameness of her nursing-home peers—just one egg among a crateful. Yet, whoever remains when the sculpting is done, I must find a way to single her out and to love her more than ever.

—Barbara Shine

slings that new mothers use these days, my medical techno-toy, a Holter monitor, snuggles between my breasts, and it will carefully record, for 24 hours, the tiniest electrical impulses of my every heartbeat. '…Oh, Lordy, how my heart grows weary….'

Tomorrow Dr. Shaw, the cardiologist, will have the Holter EKG printout and, I hope, a better idea of what comes next. She has already told me I'll need another mitral valve, next time a plastic one, "in the not-too-distant future." Oh, and by the way, my aortic valve is leaking a little, too. .

On the bright side, a spanking new mitral valve prosthesis could reduce the episodes of atrial fibrillation. But we want to put off the surgery as long as possible: Dr. Shaw wants to make sure the next valve replacement will be my last, and I'm afraid of trading the frantic bongo beats of Planet Drum for endless silence.

Lost Days
By Therese Keane

Morning

Morning is my enemy. I feel heavy and cramped, eyes deadened by insomnia. The nausea rears up as I lean over the bathroom sink to begin my medley of dry heaves, a side effect of the antidepressants and sleeping drugs that don't work.

The shower wakes me up a bit. Half-dressed, I weigh myself—112 pounds. No new loss, but no gains, either. For the past two months, I've been exhausted by lack of sleep, which in turn makes me lethargic and more sleepy. When I'm sleepy, I don't want to eat. I've lost 25 pounds.

My body moves like molasses down the three flights of stairs from the bedroom to the kitchen. On the second floor I greet my husband, Otho, working at his computer. He gets up to hug me, searching my face for a change. I tell him I'll buzz on the intercom when breakfast is ready.

I have no appetite and try to think of ways to get some nourishment. But I can't even manage cereal this morning; I choke down one piece of dry toast with a cup of tea and some juice. Otho doesn't mind that I no longer prepare nutritious breakfasts; he rarely ate breakfast before we married, less than 10 years ago, but I worry that he, too, will lose weight and get depressed because of me.

After breakfast, I am exhausted and want to nap. My days consist of how many hours I can legitimately wait before I can lie down and sleep. I ask my family and friends, "Will I get better?" Their answer is always a resounding "Yes," sometimes followed by, "if you want to."

My internist is Dr. Diamond, a gentle, quiet man in his 60s. Searching for a physical cause for my symptoms, he orders abdominal and pelvic sonograms, an upper GI series, various MRIs, and a brain scan.

His news is both good and bad. "There's nothing physically wrong with you," he says. "I think it's depression." I had hoped for a physical cause that could be named, treated, and cured. Depression is a wily, insidious beast that feels like a living death.

The Psychiatrist

"Come in, Ms. Keane," Dr. O'Connor welcomes me in a brisk, businesslike manner, without the warm comfort I had hoped for. He is prissy, tall and thin, in his late 40s, with a short mustache that reminds me of Hitler, but he had been highly recommended by two doctors. He explains he no longer participates with my medical plan. I agree to pay him in full because I know my insurance will cover six sessions. He takes out his pad. I begin talking.

"I feel like the glass is not only half-empty, it's also dirty and has a bug floating in it." He silently nods in a practiced manner, occasionally looking up from jotting in his pad. I explain how I have everything—a great husband, friends, money, and a lifestyle most people would envy—but I no longer feel anything except guilt because I don't care about any of it.

"It's like you're at a great banquet table with delicious food, but you refuse to eat any of it," he offers. I prefer my dirty-water-and-bug metaphor, but I agree that is probably so.

After an hour, Dr. O'Connor sums up my condition in three words: "generalized anxiety disorder." He prescribes Paxil, an antidepressant, and Ambien to replace my current sleeping medication, Halcion. I feel amazingly better just having a diagnosis and a prescription, which I carefully tuck inside my bag. Although I still don't have a clear idea of what caused my depression, I am on my way to better mental health, or so I think.

But after a few days, the Paxil and Ambien have no effect on my mood or my sleeping. I call Dr. O'Connor to review the medication plan. During our first visit, he had advised me to try different dosages of each drug. Start small, add half a tablet when needed. But I didn't know how to tell if either medication was working or remember which prescription to increase or decrease. Much of what he had told me had evaporated. When he returns my call, Dr. O'Connor is surprisingly abrupt: "I told you, Ms. Keane, it takes several weeks for the drugs to kick in. You just need to experiment with the dosages. I don't have time in my schedule to see you."

I panic at the idea of self-dosing with mind-altering drugs. Suppose I take too much of the

Autism

It was a sunny Monday, and I was washing the dishes with my sunglasses on.

Why? you might ask.

Well, there I was, trying to grab a few minutes for dishwashing, when my 20-month-old son handed me sunglasses to put on. I wiped my hands and put them on. We both laughed. I took them off and laid them on the counter.

He handed them to me again with a little shake of his hand. I put them on again, and he laughed, delighted. I took them off, but now he grabbed the glasses and thrust them at me determinedly. I had to finish the goddamn dishes in sunglasses.

On some rainy days I wash the dishes with my Australian rain hat on.

—Maria Hogan Pereira

wrong drug? Will I get hopelessly addicted, requiring larger doses? Finally, he suggests a more exact dosage regimen to follow.

"Sorry, could you repeat that?" I ask, trying to write it down.

Dr. O'Connor quickly shouts out the dosage, then slams the phone in my ear. Perhaps he is only trying to save me money, since psychiatrists do charge fees for phone consultations after a certain amount of time. But my ear is ringing.

At that point, I should recognize that I am with the wrong doctor, but instead I let myself feel guilty about not being patient with the medications. Eventually Dr. O'Connor changes my antidepressant prescription from Paxil to Remeron, which I take for six weeks, and recommends Zyprexa, a tranquilizer to help my anxiety about not sleeping. I am still groggy and not regaining the lost weight.

After four months, I'm still not sleeping. The meds aren't working, and I am afraid I'll turn into Judy Garland or Marilyn Monroe, popping too many pills.

"I've gone through all the meds, there's nothing more I can do for you," Dr. O'Connor says. He suggests I meet with a cognitive therapist who might help me sleep and alleviate the depression by using behavioral changes. He is dumping me.

Afternoon

I sign up for a yoga class at the YMCA. Ra, the instructor, tries to guide my rigid body into gentle poses and my mind into calm, reflective thinking. It is difficult to follow his simple instructions because my mind is so foggy.

"Don't push too hard. Just do what you can do. It'll come later," he assures me.

My sister Eileen is taking the class with me, and afterward I tell her I am no better. She says repeatedly, "You will be." We stop and look at the swimmers in the YMCA pool. It is comforting somehow to watch their strokes, each swimmer with a different style—some smooth and regular, others jerky and splashing.

After leaving the Y, we go to lunch and I try to sip some soup. The smell of food and the sight of other diners forking large portions into their mouths nauseate me. My head hurts and I want to take a nap before dinner.

The Cognitive Therapist

"You know I'm not a psychologist or psychiatrist. I'm not a talk therapist. Do you know what cognitive-behavioral therapy is?" I had a vague idea, but I let Dr. Marsh explain it.

"CBT teaches a person how to change behavioral patterns and ways of thinking that reinforce depression or phobias."

Dr. Marsh is in her 30s, no nonsense and intensely focused. She doesn't jot down a lot of interview notes, but prefers to draw circles within circles outlining the different kinds of thought processes to show how they interact to affect behavior.

"You need to change your automatic 'hot' thoughts, or negative thoughts, into more balanced thoughts to see the situation in a better light."

To help change my NATs (negative automatic thoughts) to ABTs (alternative balanced thoughts), Dr. Marsh assigns me a workbook with weekly "Thought Record" exercise sheets to fill out. The idea is to describe a situation that prompts a negative thought or behavior, and then find evidence that either supports or does not support that negative thought. After going through the exercise, I should discover an alternative, or more balanced, thought that shows that the situation is not as bad as I had originally believed. For example:

My negative hot thought might be: I'll never be able to sleep again.

The evidence supporting this thought is: I haven't slept in months.

The evidence that doesn't support it: I used to be able to sleep.

The balanced thought: With the right meds, exercise, and therapy, I will be able to sleep again.

I could see the value of CBT, but I was too tired to struggle with the "evidence" columns and found myself dozing over my workbook. The CBT is a limited form of therapy and is most effective in the early stages of depression. I had been depressed for four months when I started the cognitive therapy. If CBT doesn't work after eight or more sessions, the therapist bounces the patient back to the doctor. Dr. Marsh said goodbye to me.

"But do call me in the future for any 'brush up' sessions."

Evening

My mood lifts a bit as the sun sets. I am less fatigued—perhaps because of all the daytime naps necessitated by my nighttime insomnia. During these dusk hours I feel almost normal as the depression briefly goes into hibernation. But at dinner, my anxiety rises when I notice a calendar and several invitations sitting next to Otho's plate. Social situations, which I once anticipated with joy, now paralyze me. I cannot focus on conversations unless they revolve around my depression—a topic I can share only with family and selected friends.

"How are you feeling?" Otho gently asks.

"About the same, maybe a little better," I say.

His expression remains steadfast as he struggles to hide disappointment, which will only make me feel guiltier.

I silently reminisce about how I once enjoyed going out, meeting new people and drinking wine (alcohol is forbidden now because of the antidepressant medication). That joyful person seems gone forever.

As I wind down in front of the TV, I find it hard to focus on program story lines. Ads for Paxil and Ambien—meds that failed me—magically produce TV actors who go from glum to giddy after ingesting their pills. I switch off the set and go to bed, now wide awake.

The Psychologist

The monster inside me insists I will never feel whole and happy again. I am guilty, angry, helpless, selfish, dumb, lazy, immature, empty, and exhausted. I cannot find a psychiatrist who will both prescribe drugs *and* meet me for weekly therapy. After the disastrous Dr. O'Connor, I call two other psychiatrists—both women. They tell me they can meet with me once a month to monitor my drugs, but I need to find someone else for regular therapy. This apparently is the norm, not the exception. I tell them thanks, but I really need a therapist. One of them recommends a psychologist.

Dr. Nelson is a woman around 40 with an open, welcoming face. She empathizes with me and offers tissues when I break down in tears. The cry, the first one I've had since the depression began six months ago, is magnificently cleansing and refreshing.

"You have an illness; it's not your fault." Her goal is to help me focus on places and activities I used to enjoy. But when I think of those old happy times, I become more depressed because I can't enjoy them anymore.

Nevertheless, I listen to the custom-made audiotape she's recorded for me. It's a hypnotic pep talk incorporating information she gleaned from questions and answers in our first session: My favorite season (spring); the swing set that gave me joy as a child as I soared up and down; long walks on the beach on breezy days.

Her quiet voice is soothing, encouraging, and hopeful: "Take a deep breath…and release. Imagine the sound of the ocean. You are walking along the shore. The sun is warm on your face, the sand cool under your feet…."

Although those happy moments from my past are now alien and fleeting, I continue to listen to the tape, hoping that it will heal at some subconscious level as time goes on. Dr. Nelson tells me repeatedly that I'll get better.

"Depression usually lifts after six to nine months," she assures me. So I have three months to go, I tell myself. I don't know if I can make it.

The Psychopharmacologist

"Call Dr. Goldman *today!*" Dr. Diamond, my normally calm internist, shouts into my telephone ear. After a series of failed antidepressants and sedatives with no weight gain, I am spiraling downward. Dr. Diamond insists I see Dr.

Goldman, a psychiatrist who specializes in prescribing drugs. I reluctantly make the appointment.

Dr. Goldman is a short, curly-haired, fast-moving man in his 30s. He appears almost breathless from moving so quickly to escort me from the lobby to his office. During our 50-minute meeting, he reviews my history of failed antidepressants, listens to my problems, and writes copious notes as Dr. O'Connor, my first psychiatrist, had done. At the end of our session he prescribes a new antidepressant called Lexapro, which he feels will help me but will take the usual few weeks to kick in.

"I can't wait any longer," I plead. "I'm ready for electroshock therapy because I know that's faster."

"You would still need to be on antidepressants before ECT and continue on them after. And the ECT sessions themselves will take two weeks. Let's try the Lexapro first," he said.

He quickly escorts me out the door. I leave his office, discouraged and hopeless, clutching another new prescription in my hand.

The Upward Curve

After two months of taking Lexapro, my psychologist notices an improvement, although I still don't quite feel it.

"You are better; I can see it," Dr. Nelson says earnestly.

My crying jags in her office are less frequent. I am not sure if I am better or just adjusting to my depression. I'm coming up to that magical ninth-month deadline when the depression is supposed to lift.

I create daily activity lists to describe the hours from the time I get up until I go to bed. Some days are better; others feel like I am rolling down into the familiar abyss. The winter months are ending. I can smell spring in the air.

I sign up for more yoga classes at the YMCA. Ra uses me as an example to encourage a new student in the class who is having problems.

"Don't worry, Mary. Therese could barely move when she was in my class last session. She's so much better now!"

I feel alternately embarrassed and proud, but realize other people are seeing improvements that I am still blind to. My sister grins on the yoga mat beside me.

My appetite is light, but I work on eating small amounts of food several times a day. It's easier than trying to absorb three full meals.

Dr. Goldman, the psychopharmacologist, is adjusting the dosage of the Lexapro and the Zyprexa—but sometimes I have a hard time remembering how much of which drug to take. When he becomes impatient with me, I surprise myself by offering a new response to his hurried approach.

The cognitive-behavioral therapist, Dr. Marsh, had told me to be more assertive with doctors if I felt they weren't listening to me. With a trembling voice, I take Dr. Goldman on: "Look, the depression is making me anxious about these drugs. I've been on a lot of them, and I need some support in getting them straight and understanding the dosages and how long they will take to have an effect. It's hard for me to remember." To my amazement, Dr. Goldman is more attentive and doesn't rush me off the phone.

Perhaps this is progress.

I start to accept invitations to parties and other events with friends, although I am still frozen and crippled by any interaction with people I don't know. I feel mute but struggle to make small talk. It is agonizing.

Dr. Nelson applauds and smiles broadly at any bit of progress I make. I feel like a baby taking first steps. Again and again, she reminds me that depression is an illness, not something I should feel guilty about: "Think of it like diabetes. You need to take medication to control it."

The depression is lifting—along with the guilt.

Epilogue

My depression took the full nine months to lift. That was over three years ago, and so far, I haven't had a recurrence. I still take Lexapro every day. Although I still have trouble sleeping, I'm much less anxious about it. My emotions are a bit dulled by the medication, but it's insignificant compared to the debilitating effects of depression. Dr. Goldman warns that relapses into depression are usually worse than earlier episodes, so I'm not taking any chances.

And the cause of the depression? Hard to say. Part of it may have been adjusting to a first marriage at the age of 46, and the loss of a professional career that petered out. Marriage gave me the luxury of not needing a job, but I no longer had a connection to an outside community of work and colleagues. The onset of menopause also robbed me of those nights of deep, uninterrupted sleep from my youth.

I'm now back to a comfortable social life and find that I enjoy parties but still value my solo time. A lot of the invitations get tossed (without guilt) because I'd rather stay home, read or watch TV, have a quiet dinner with my husband, or go out with my old girlfriends.

But I don't believe my depression should have taken nine months. So much time was spent struggling to find the right combination of help—the doctor, the therapist, the drugs—at a time when my mental and physical energies were significantly impaired.

I no longer feel guilty, but I am angry because I lost so many days that I will never get back.

Seeking the Zen in Bowling
By Lori Carruthers

Bowling is my favorite meditation. It is personal, private—the ball, the pins, and me. It is my opportunity to achieve the nirvana of watching all the pins tumble down, or at least some of them. A way to seek understanding as I observe from a measured distance the outcome of my actions.

I am a mediocre bowler, happy if I break 100—far from the perfection of 300. Nevertheless, I am happy to be bowling, to hear the clatter of pins scattering, as I aim for that next strike.

I do not bowl in large groups; however, I enjoy time spent with friends at my favorite alley. I appreciate the camaraderie that spills across the lanes to those one might otherwise call strangers. Newfound friends have given me advice and readily shared their insights. They guide me in understanding the finer points, like how many steps to take or at what point to swing my arm as I strive to perfect my technique.

Occasionally I will see someone bowling by himself; more than likely he is already a master, using the solitude to improve upon himself and his score, and bring his playing to a higher level. One quiet weekday afternoon, I watched a guy bowl with five different balls. Each was scored as a separate player, as if he and that particular ball were their own persona, seeking excellence with each unique ball and its distinctive balance.

On a family outing to a bowling alley, my brother-in-law Jim surprised me with his skill and flair. He is over 60 and has a slight, unathletic build. He gently strolled to the foul line and smoothly swung his ball toward the pins, which came crashing down moments after he finished his follow-through with a flourish and a little kick. We youngsters, with our awkward and inconsistent moves, could not approach his steady mastery.

More recently, I have gone bowling on Sunday mornings with my friend Mike, not just for the off-peak prices, but also for the quiet. Sunday morning is a time when most lanes are empty. It's my opportunity to tally whether my mind and body are working in harmony, unobserved by aggressive players. I use my bowling score as a measure of my personal progress, not as a judgment of my ability.

I know what it takes for me to bowl a strike, but never attain it consistently. My quest on these Sunday mornings is to maintain my focus and to achieve a score higher than the last. To find the moment of harmony, when my action and desire are in accord.

I step up to the line, my timing and concentration guiding my actions. The pace of my steps is my own, no need to coordinate with the person in the next lane. No worries about interfering with her peripheral vision or concentration, as most lanes are still empty at this early hour.

My friend Mike and I fall into a natural rhythm, watching each other's form and affirming each other's accomplishments. Our personalities become more pronounced in this environment. Mike throws the ball with full force of his weight behind him. The 13-pound ball bounces down the alley, pins falling and tumbling from the energy of his throw. He seems to flatten all of them through his will and strength, the same way he walks through life, unhesitating and without caution. I am embarrassed by the noise and fearful that his ball will scar the smooth wood as it careens down the lane to the waiting pins. As the ball strikes them, there is no indecision; the momentum of pins falling tumbles those around the edges into obedience. His method is not perfect: There are times when the ball bounces down the empty gutter with the same vigor with which he scores a strike.

I gently roll, not throw, a much lighter ball, reminding myself to aim for the center arrows marked on the lane and follow through with my arm and wrist straight up, not twisting to the side—my formula for bowling a strike. I follow these rules and seek power through consistency, not strength. The thought of an artificial device to keep my wrist straight does not appeal to me. I want to do it on my own.

Sometimes I measure my stride. Standing at the line with my back to the pins, I hold the ball in my two hands, left fingers in the holes, right hand cradling the bottom. I take two steps away from the pins. I turn, then step, step, genuflect, lower the ball and gently release it, my hand sweeping past my knee as I follow through.

Other times, I stand at the foul line holding the ball, focusing forward, on the center, on the task before me as I release the ball. Usually I know the outcome as soon as I let go. When I do well, I try to memorize the moment and hold that feeling inside, aiming for the day when concentration and form are integrated with my desire.

When I do badly and the ball skitters down the gutter, I hover over the ball return, impatiently waiting for the machine to spit it back out at me. I stand still as I watch the mechanical bar fall and sweep all the pins down and away. I second-guess myself and wonder if I should seek a lighter or, perhaps, a heavier ball. Or try again with the same sphere to improve the outcome. My decisions echo my inconsistencies.

Building upon success, combining spares and strikes, I know my score will soar. I know I will one day achieve a "turkey," three strikes in a row. More often, my isolated triumphs—scoring a single strike sandwiched by gutter balls—leave me with a flatter total. I can go from gutter ball to strike, back to gutter ball, and then making the spare on a difficult split within less time than it takes me to lace up my rented shoes. Triumph and failure side by side.

I know the formula for success and have used it with great results. However, the minutest break in my concentration produces a disaster, my ball lurching toward the gutter instead of the number 1 pin.

What keeps me coming back is this: I know that no matter how awful one frame is, I have the skill and possibility of achieving a spare or a strike in the next. The X on my scorecard, a symbol of perfection, encourages me to try again. Looking for excellence in the next frame. Trying to learn from the past.

St. Jude and the Tell-Tale Heart
By Barbara Shine

Photo: Sam Kittner, copyright 2006; used with permission

Literature is full of hearts, both real and metaphorical: *Heart of Darkness, Bury My Heart at Wounded Knee, Hearts in Atlantis.* But my favorite has always been Edgar Allan Poe's story, "The Tell-Tale Heart." In Poe's taut story, a murderer is haunted, and finally forced to confess, by the sound of his victim's heartbeat persisting long after the fatal act. And I think of that story almost every day, when my own heart startles me with its tick-tick-ticking.

Several years ago, my cardiologists at George Washington University found that my mitral valve, transplanted from the heart of a large pig, was calcifying—growing stiff—and no longer working as it should. I felt fatigue, shortness of breath, and frightening irregular heart rhythms. The specialists then worried me further by recommending another open-heart surgery, to implant a device called the St. Jude Mechanical Valve. I had heard of the St. Jude valve, but never thought it was for me. After all, Jude is the patron saint of impossible causes, right? I couldn't be *that* sick!

But it turns out that St. Jude is the name of the company that *makes* the valve; it's *not* named to be the valve of last resort. Still, it seemed an unnecessarily cruel twist for an already-weakened heart patient: "Yours is a tough case. We'll have to bring in St. Jude."

The phrase "hopeless cause" nagged at me for weeks. And even now, friends who customarily turn to the intercession of saints look at me with concern when I mention my St. Jude heart valve.

My doctors did prepare me for the surgery's most notable aftereffect: Unlike the mitral valve I was born with and the porcine valve I carried for nine years, the St. Jude valve, made of lightweight metals and plastic, is noisy. They said the valve would last the rest of my life, and I'd get used to the noise.

The valve ticks and clicks like a cheap watch. But the thing is not cheap; it cost thousands to make and install. The surgeon's skill is priceless. You'd think the implanted valve, a showpiece of biomedical engineering, would sound more resonant and ponderously drumlike, more deep and important than the Timex counter at Kmart.

I hear the valve mostly in the morning, after I shuffle from bed to bath. In the predawn quiet, with no distractions, and before taking the heart medicine that controls rhythm, I marvel at the noise: It's a troupe of tiny flamenco dancers under my nightgown! And it sounds like the beginners' class—flailing away on their tinny castanets in a dysrhythmic frenzy, trying to find a consistent pace.

At night, the noisy valve can keep me awake. Sometimes it's just too loud; other nights it keeps reminding me of its presence and lifesaving work, and I can't help wondering: What if I *stop* hearing it? It's been totally, noisily reliable for years, but what if it goes quiet?

During the workday, my noisy valve is less intrusive. Or maybe I'm just too busy to notice. But sometimes a muffled ticking breaks through the clicks of my computer keyboard. And automatically I look down at my left wrist. After all this time, and knowing full well what that clicking noise is, I still foolishly bring my arm up in front of my face and ask, "What is *wrong* with this watch?"

Then I remember St. Jude and Edgar Allan Poe and the sound he said was "like a clock wrapped in cotton." And I recognize the noise is not the ticking of my watch but the beating of my own tell-tale heart.

Painted Alphabet
By Julie Link Haifley

Amethyst auburn apricot
Beige butterscotch bronze brick

Crimson cobalt celadon cream
Daffodil dandelion drab dove

Emerald eggshell ebony ecru
Fuchsia forest forget-me-not flax

Golden garnet geranium grape
Hyacinth hazel heather hemp

Ivory iris indigo ice
Jonquil jasmine jade

Kiwi khaki kumquat
Lavender lapis lime

Magenta mauve mahogany mint
Nasturtium navy nectarine nut

Olive oyster orchid oak
Persimmon puce pumpkin pearl

Quercitron quinone quince
Ruby raven russet rose

Saffron scarlet sapphire smoke
Tangerine turquoise topaz taupe

Ultramarine umber urochrome
Vermilion vanilla verdigris
Wisteria walnut wine wheat

Xanthin
Yellow
Zaffer zinc

Chapter 6

Candles, Ribbons, and Champagne

Birthday Greetings From New Orleans
By Therese Keane

*It was 25 years ago when I made my first, and only, visit to New Orleans—
a quarter-century before Hurricane Katrina did. The following story
explores the city I experienced in 1980, a city that has been altered by both
the natural cycle of two decades of change and the almost supernatural disaster of Hurricane Katrina in September 2005.*

I wanted to get out of town on my 30th birthday. For me, the city of Washington
had the sex appeal of a balding man who parts his hair over his left ear and thinks
"formal" means putting on a tie with his short-sleeve shirt. I thought about
another city—Paris, which I had visited when I was 21. That city was built for
romance. Stylishly dressed lovers could stroll leisurely through a lush garden or
talk undisturbed for hours in a sidewalk café. I fondly remembered two young
men, Christian and Robert, who flipped a coin to see who would serenade me
along the Seine near Notre Dame. And the food—I can still taste the hot croissants and café au lait I savored every morning.

But could I recreate that kind of Paris 10 years later? Probably not. Besides, I
couldn't afford the plane ticket on my meager public radio salary. And I couldn't
count on meeting the likes of Christian and Robert again.

My good friend Susan came up with an alternate idea.

"Why don't we go to New Orleans for your birthday weekend?" she offered.
"They speak French, it's not that far away, and I've always wanted to go there. I
know I'm not exactly the person you had in mind to travel with, but we can have
a good time. How about it?"

I envisioned New Orleans—the land of jazz musicians and Bourbon Street;
mouth-watering Cajun and Creole food, including those famous beignets; and
the charming trolley cars, a reminder of more civilized traffic from an earlier
time. Susan would be a good travel companion. She liked to party but also had a
good heart and the common sense of a New Englander. Besides, I would turn 30
only once, and a weekend in New Orleans had to be better than staying home or
sharing another obligatory birthday dinner with well-meaning friends.

"Okay. Let's go!" I said.

My travel-savvy acquaintances confirmed my high expectations of the city and
recommended a restaurant to celebrate my birthday dinner. Susan and I would
economize by staying with Vee and Fred Sheehan, friends of my sister's. We were
on our way.

We arrived in New Orleans on my birthday—a sunny Saturday in November. After dropping off our bags, we barely greeted our hosts before changing into jeans and T-shirts and heading downtown. In the center of the city, we discovered a boisterous parade traveling down the main street. We joined the crowd cheering the antics of clowns and admired the floats bedecked with waving young girls overdressed in poufy, pastel gowns. We weren't sure what the parade was for, but the prevailing mood of the college-age onlookers suggested a football game and homecoming event.

Suddenly, I saw a woman across the street looking distraught and waving frantically in our direction. I didn't know her, so I assumed she was trying to get someone else's attention. But she continued to point at us. When there was a break between the cowboys on horseback and the paddlewheel riverboat float, she dashed across the street and headed straight toward me.

"I was trying to warn you," she shouted, out of breath. "A man was standing behind you, and I think he took your wallet out of your purse."

My head jerked toward my shoulder bag. The zipper was open. The wallet was gone. Susan shot out of the crowd.

"Let's go get him," she said, running in the direction the woman pointed. We pursued an unseen thief for about three blocks, but found no one who matched the man's description.

There I stood, with no money, credit cards, or identification. I had been in New Orleans less than an hour.

In spite of my loss, I had to admire the fleet fingers of that silent thief. Of course, I never felt a thing amid all the jostling of the parade watchers. But why did he choose me? I felt like a naïve, dumb tourist—something right out of an old American Express commercial with Karl Malden's words ringing in my ear: "What will you do? What *will* you do?"

"I've got my American Express card," Susan reassured me.

I felt dazed and violated as I gazed inside my purse containing nothing now but a lonely compact and lipstick staring back at me.

We wandered around the quaint streets and stopped to watch a young black dancer. Accompanied by a boom box, he strutted and tapped in a style that embraced both Michael Jackson and Bill "Bojangles" Robinson. He performed under a lacy, wrought-iron balcony that watched over him like an elegant grandmother from a different century. I noticed a cap full of coins and started to unzip my purse. Then I remembered and slowly zipped the purse closed.

No other musicians appeared on any streets we strolled. No soulful jazz saxophonist. No spirited Dixieland funeral procession playing "When the Saints Go Marchin' In."

We did see many liquor stores, however, and decided to buy champagne for our hosts. The clerk pointed to a row of bottles topped with gold foil. They were carefully balanced, like acrobats in a pyramid.

Susan removed one of the bottles. As she turned away, the pyramid suddenly began to move and quickly rearranged itself into a single assembly line of rapidly moving bombs. As each bottle hit the floor, it exploded, showering us with foamy liquid and shards of green glass and shooting corks that ricocheted around the store.

"…25, 50," Susan was calculating our bill as each bottle burst. A small flood of champagne suds pooled around our feet. The clerk rushed over and threw his body over the rolling bottles.

"We're so sorry! I don't know how it happened—they seemed so secure. We just removed one bottle," I apologized and tried to help the clerk contain the movement.

"…75, 100," Susan was still calculating in an eerie trance.

"That's okay, don't worry about these," said the clerk, straddling the rest of the bottles. "Just take this one, and pay for it." He handed us a rescued Korbel. "And please be careful—don't slip on the wet floor on your way out."

We tiptoed around the glass on our way to the cashier, paid, and quickly left.

Clutching our bottle in its safe brown bag, we hailed a trolley to go home. As we sat down, the passengers near us frowned, then got up and moved to other seats. We smelled as if we had fallen into a vat of booze.

When we arrived home, Susan reminded me we were having my birthday dinner at Chez Lafitte, one of the best French restaurants in New Orleans.

"After a fabulous feast—where we'll be *drinking* champagne instead of wearing it—we'll hit Bourbon Street and hear some great jazz," she assured me. I felt

Found Object

My sister is an English teacher in Japan. For my birthday, she sent me part of an old dresser she found on a garbage heap. The gold chrysanthemums scattered on black lacquer are faded, the tiny drawers behind dollhouse-sized doors smell musty. But I treasure the wooden box for what Nini put into it. She papered the inside with photos from our childhood, happy smiling pictures of our parents, my children growing up. My jewelry now rests on time capsules from the past. Yesterday I heard a radio commentator talk about "found object art." Mine is a found object from the heart.

—Julia Weller

hopeful as I wiped away the grime of the day's experience and changed into a slinky dress of daffodil yellow silk. Renewed in spirit, we headed for Chez Lafitte.

The restaurant exuded French style, understated but elegant, full of starched white tablecloths. A single pink rose stood centered on each table. The walls were covered in a blue-gray fabric that provided the background for tasteful prints of pirate ships and paddlewheel boats. A large portrait of a dashing pirate, dressed in black and white with a bejeweled sword at his side, surveyed the dining area. Jean Lafitte, the French pirate who helped Andrew Jackson drive the British from New Orleans in 1815, watched Susan and me as we sank into the floral fabric of high-backed chairs.

The obsequious staff, in stiff white shirts and bow ties rather than pirate head scarves and ear hoops, offered us a menu that featured both French and Cajun cuisine.

Susan had the seafood jambalaya, with shrimp and mussels steeped in garlic sauce. She pronounced it a great success.

I discovered that most of the Cajun menu involved shellfish, one of my allergies. So I opted for a favorite meat dish—filet mignon. It was cooked precisely to my specification.

After the plates were removed, our waiter asked if we would like some dessert.

Susan frowned and whispered something in his ear. He looked puzzled, then nodded and quickly returned to the kitchen.

Several minutes later, a trio of waiters led a procession from the kitchen into the dining room. They were carefully guarding something on a tray. I could make out the flickering light of a candle.

When they arrived at our table, they burst into the "Happy Birthday" song. I looked at the special dessert.

Lying on the tray were two baguettes of French bread fused together into the body and head of some kind of bird. On the top of one loaf, a white paper lace doily perched like a little chapel veil and held a small, white twinkling candle in its center. A long dill pickle protruded from the side of the bread to form the profile of a beak. Two beady green olives peeked out above the pickle. I looked at it. It stared back at me, candle wax dripping into its olives. I looked at Susan. Her eyes froze on the bird and her mouth fell open. She shook her head in despair, put her elbows on the table, and dropped her face into her hands.

I looked at the waiters. They were beaming.

"We made it especially for you, mademoiselle—for your special birthday. It is a Toucan bird!" They waited for a response.

"Why, it's just—ah—well—very *special!*" I said, trying to look pleased. I wanted them to go away and take the bird with them.

They left, leaving the dessert bird with us and, I assume, congratulating themselves on making the best of their mistake—forgetting Susan's original dessert request.

"I called the restaurant before we left Washington and ordered a chocolate mousse cake. We discussed it in detail. I can't believe it!" Susan was near tears.

"Maybe they thought the bird would be better than a mousse cake. Maybe it's some kind of New Orleans birthday tradition, you know—giving the bird to someone when she turns 30," I said, trying to cheer my friend.

We both looked at the bird again for a long time in silence. Then we burst out laughing. A few patrons came by to admire the birthday bird sculpture.

"Wherever did you get such a clever idea?" asked one diner.

"It was a surprise from the restaurant," I said, as cheerfully as I could.

After ordering some éclairs, we left the restaurant—and the bird—to venture to Bourbon Street. I was finally going to hear some authentic New Orleans jazz. But as we walked down that historic passageway, we were surrounded by hordes of drunken college boys. Unfortunately, these Louisiana Lotharios hadn't quite learned the skill of holding their liquor and other bodily fluids until they reached their own rooms. The stench proved that Bourbon Street was aptly named.

"Therese, I now believe we've died and gone to hell," Susan observed.

We left Bourbon Street, hailed a cab, and returned to the safety of our hosts' home. We opened the unbroken bottle of champagne and rolled up the living room rug for dancing. Susan sat down at the piano, while Vee and I took turns twirling around the floor with Fred, a great dancer. We played Scott Joplin and tunes from "Showboat," and we sang our own version of "When the Saints Come Marchin' In."

New Orleans did come through for me on my 30th birthday—not quite as I imagined that birthday would be, but certainly making it an unforgettable weekend. It is famous, and for me, one of the most infamous cities in the world.

And I still get birthday cards featuring Toucan birds from my New Orleans hosts—who now live in Maine.

Holiday Blues (fiction)
By Allyson Denise Walker

Nina sat on the sofa wrapped in a blanket, slouched so far down her head was barely visible. She was eating a pint of Ben and Jerry's chocolate chip cookie dough ice cream and watching a "That Girl" marathon on television. It wasn't easy to ignore the unsettling combination of guilt and worry that came from squandering her savings on expensive ice cream and cable TV. She had no idea how long her savings would last. But the ice cream and the blue flickering light that reflected on her face produced enough of a stupor to help her forget her troubles, if only for a few moments.

Ten weeks ago she'd been managing corporate accounts at a large investment firm. Now she was commuting to TV Land with a click of the remote. Nina knew she should have been spending her time polishing her resume and writing cover letters but it was almost more than she could bear. How could she look at a one-page summary of 20 years of hard work, including her bachelor's degree and MBA, knowing she was going to end up on the sofa with no one but Marlo Thomas to keep her company?

The telephone rang, jerking her out of her daze. She let the answering machine pick up—probably one of those telemarketers—but it was worse than that.

"Hello, Nina, this is your mother." Nina groaned. "I hope you're out on an interview. I was just calling to remind you of your date with Frances Wright's son. You might want to touch up your roots, they were looking a little nappy last time I saw you. And wear your black skirt. It's slimming. Love you." *Beep.*

Cursing her judgment for agreeing to go on a blind date arranged by her own mother, Nina got up. It had gotten dark while she was watching TV, and she tripped over her running shoes on her way to the bathroom. She peered into the jar of relaxer cream. There was enough for two more applications if she really stretched it.

Two hours later she was powdered and perfumed, her hair tamed into a sleek pageboy, and her almost size-12 body squeezed into her size-10 black skirt. She made a mental note to order salad for dinner. She couldn't afford to outgrow her clothes.

*   *   *

Driving to the restaurant revived Nina's worries about making car payments. No new Lexus this year—she'd be driving a 20th century Toyota before spring.

She would not be reduced to riding the bus. Without a car it would be next to impossible to get to interviews on time. Not that she'd been on any interviews.

The restaurant was full of lively, well-dressed people in pairs or groups. Feeling conspicuously alone, Nina approached the bar. Fortified with a glass of water with lemon and a menu, she perched on a stool and tried to look casually confident. All of the names of the dishes were in Italian and originated in Naples or Tuscany or Venice. Everything looked wonderful, but she was sure she could eat canned spaghetti for dinner for two solid weeks for the cost of tonight's meal.

"Nina James?"

She looked up into the face of Frances Wright's son. What was his name, she wondered in a panic? Robert? Randall?

"Ron Wright," he said smoothly, holding out his hand. Nina automatically extended hers. His handshake was warm and firm, and his eyes were friendly. "Let's find a table," he said.

Nina attempted a graceful slide off her stool and landed a little too hard on one foot. Ron caught her by the elbow but released her as they threaded their way back to the seating hostess. Moments later they were seated in a booth with fresh glasses of water with lemon and a plate of Italian bread with a small carafe of olive oil.

Pleasant was the word she came up with to describe him as she answered his polite questions about her preferences in food, films, and music. He was good-looking in an ordinary sort of way, with his close, corporate haircut and charcoal pinstripe suit. He looked like the sort of man who paid his taxes on time, almost never drove more than 10 miles over the speed limit, and would probably not try anything more than a couple of kisses (maybe with a little tongue) on the first date.

Nina found his predictability soothing. She knew he'd prefer playing golf to basketball, jazz to hip-hop, and the "New York Times" book review section to actual books. She even knew he'd order the spaghetti carbonara. Nina forgot her promise to the mirror and ordered the fettuccine alfredo.

Halfway through the meal, however, she began to notice Ron glancing over her shoulder and checking his watch. He was bored. Bored! She felt as though he'd dumped his glass of ice water over her head. He was pleasant and polite but after 55 minutes of small talk with a woman with no job and 20 extra pounds, he was ready to move on. She was incapable of holding a man's attention unless she was trying to sell him securities and she no longer had that privilege. Nina wished she could pick up her remote control and make him vanish with the push of a button.

"Look," she said, leaning forward suddenly. "Let's just stop this nonsense. I don't want to waste any more of your time. It's not like we're going to end up in bed or anything. I don't do sex on the first date anymore—too dangerous. It wasn't your idea go out with me, anyway—a woman with no job and no money to buy the henna rinse to cover my gray." She brushed impatiently at her temples. "I'm sure you'd rather be with someone younger and sexier, and I could be at home watching my 'Spider Man 2' DVD…"

"You have 'Spider Man 2' on DVD?"

Nina was gathering up her purse and jacket. "So let's just quit while we're ahead, okay?" She slid out of the booth. "It was nice meeting you. Thanks for dinner."

She walked away without looking back, but her pride melted once she turned the corner. She touched the sleeve of the nearest waiter and asked to have her dinner boxed up. She paced in front of the door where she got a fresh blast of November chill every time a laughing, chatting couple came in. When the server finally brought her bag, she caught a glimpse of Ron near the bar putting his arms around a slim brown woman with hair like a Dark and Lovely ad. It figured.

*   *   *

The mall was decked out with tinsel, lights, and artificial greenery, and it wasn't even Thanksgiving. Nina wasn't there to shop. She'd grown tired of her diet of Top Ramen and ice cream and wanted to be able to afford a few Christmas gifts this year. She'd tugged on the same black skirt she'd worn on her disastrous date with Frances Wright's son, matched it with a black knit top and red blazer, and went to fill out department store applications. Bing Crosby's smooth baritone was being piped through the audio system, and Nina had to fight the urge to run back to her car and seek sanctuary in front of the television.

It didn't take the department store manager long to recognize a professional when she saw Nina. Nina had on her suit and best sales demeanor and was available for all shifts. She was asked to start immediately.

And so began her new career in retail—a fine way to use her MBA. At first it was demoralizing to wait on demanding, exacting customers who displayed a stunning variety of bad tempers. They could be impatient or imperious, condescending or careless. Nina was contemptuous until she remembered that she herself had been one of those customers just a short time ago. She had not been one of the unpleasant ones, but she knew her privileges as a store patron and did not hesitate to exercise them. Now she had to be consistently polite in the face of rudeness, swallowing sharp remarks, her teeth clenched behind her tight smile. It was depressing.

It was also depressing to walk the mall during her breaks, window shopping for gifts. Nina remembered how thoughtlessly she'd spent her entire paycheck on items from Nieman Marcus or Sharper Image for her family and friends. She knew it was the thought that counted, but for Nina it had been the thought that she could afford the best of everything that counted. She had impeccable taste, and everyone knew it.

But Nina discovered that department store commissions added up, and the more even-tempered and persuasive she was, the better she could afford to put the finer things under her tree. She also took a certain pride in the way management relied on her. She was no flighty college student or 20-something who hated to work weekends.

Soon she was in charge of the holiday charity project. The staff had adopted a family from the women's shelter, and Nina was gathering the employees' donations of food, clothes, toys, and household appliances.

Nina was just getting used to her new routine and the feeling of calm that accompanied it when she was startled by a familiar face approaching her counter. Frances Wright's son, looking adorably out of place in the cosmetics and jewelry section, was walking toward her. The sight of him triggered a wave of panic and embarrassment, but he'd already recognized her.

"Nina James," he said, with his pleasant, friendly smile.

"Ron Wright." She forced her saleswoman's smile and managed a hint of professional warmth in her voice. "How are you?"

"Doing well," he responded with a nod. "And yourself?"

"What better place to spend my time during the holidays?" She waved expansively at the holiday displays. "May I help you with something?"

"Yes, as a matter of fact. I'm looking for a gift for a lady friend, and I'm not sure what to get."

Naturally. Nina felt her smile freeze in place. "What did you have in mind?"

"I have no idea what sort of thing women go for these days."

'Liar,' she thought.

"What kind of gift would you choose?"

"Well, let's see…perfume is always nice." She reached for some testers. "We have a nice selection here to choose from. And you can get a boxed set of fragrance, lotion, and dusting powder."

"What scent do you prefer?" he asked.

"Ralph Lauren's Style is a good choice. It's a sophisticated floral fragrance."

"That sounds fine."

She led Ron to the register and rang up his purchase with polite small talk, her frozen smile still in place. After he was gone, Nina slipped into the employee lounge and helped herself to a couple of Hershey's miniatures wrapped in red, green, and silver foil. She hated her life.

*   *   *

As the days leading up to Christmas slipped by, Nina's savings account balance began to slow its sharp decline and finally steadied. Nina, who was working 12 hours a day, seven days a week, savored her hour in front of the television watching Christmas movies and soaking her feet. It wasn't the paycheck she was accustomed to, but it was better than nothing. What was she going to do when it all ended in January?

In the meantime, she collected a generous stash of goodies to take to the adopted family at the women's shelter. She was to make the delivery a week before Christmas, but no one (not even her manager) volunteered to help her. So she found herself alone at the shelter early on a Saturday morning, her not-so-new Lexus (in need of a good wash) loaded down with gifts.

A light brown woman in a bulky red and green sweater with her hair pulled back into a ponytail was at the front desk. When Nina explained who she was, the woman's face lit up. "Those are for me," she said. "They got me helping out now since they're short-staffed. Did you get anything for the kids?"

"Plenty of stuff for the kids," Nina assured the woman as she followed Nina to her car. She opened the trunk and the woman clasped her hands together.

"Oh, praise the Lord! This is so wonderful."

Nina shrugged and smiled. "Let's get all this stuff out of here."

They each took a box and carried them back to the front office. "It's been real hard since my husband left me," the woman explained, slightly out of breath from the weight of the boxes. "Understand, I was glad to see him go, but the money went with him, and I haven't worked in eight years. It's been just impossible to find a job."

"Don't I know it," replied Nina feelingly, setting her box down.

"Had to put my pride in my pocket when I came here," the woman continued, following Nina back out for more boxes. "I felt like I wanted to die, accepting charity. I don't need a whole lot for me and I really don't need a whole lot for my kids, but it's Christmas. You don't want to have to face your kids when you got nothing under the tree. You got any kids?" she asked Nina as they balanced the remaining boxes and struggled back through the doors of the shelter.

"No," Nina replied, "but I know how you feel. I don't really have a job, either. I'm just doing this for the holidays."

"Yeah, well, at least it's something." The woman set her boxes down. "At least you get to do something nice for someone for Christmas. That's why I don't mind doing a little work to help out around here. I kind of feel like I'm paying back something."

Nina nodded and smiled, her throat unexpectedly tight. She held out her hand. "It was nice meeting you. Good luck."

The woman squeezed her hand. "Good luck to you, too, girlfriend."

Nina got back in her car and drove away, unable to swallow her tears. They streamed down her cheeks until she had to pull over to find a tissue from the glove compartment. She blew her nose.

It wasn't supposed to be this way. She wasn't supposed to empathize with the needy, the families who were getting the Thanksgiving and Christmas baskets. She wanted to be Lady Bountiful, the sorority sister and faithful church member who worked so hard on the fundraising campaign. She wanted to drive up in her new Lexus, wearing her designer jeans and college sweatshirt, carrying the boxes carefully so as not to chip her Elizabeth Arden manicure. The worst of it was, now that she had a glimpse of what it felt like to be needy, to have to put her pride in her pocket, she still wanted the money and the status symbols. She still wanted to feel successful and superior and queen it over the poor unfortunates who had lost jobs or homes to electrical fires due to overloading the faulty wiring with holiday decorations. She didn't want to despise herself for being condescending and snobbish, but she couldn't help it.

Nina pulled into the parking lot of her apartment building and ran upstairs to wash her face and change for work. She had no time for self-pity when she had a precious paycheck to earn.

*   *   *

The week leading up to Christmas was one of the most grueling Nina had experienced. The hours were long, her feet were aching, and her spirits were sagging. But she couldn't let any of that come between her and her sales. Despite herself, Nina felt herself slipping into the old competitive mode of challenging herself with sales goals and closing the most reluctant of customers. If she had to be a sales clerk, however temporarily, she might as well make the best of it.

Still, when Christmas Eve came, she wasn't looking forward to it. The music and the decorations wore on her nerves, and she was glad to close up at 6:00. Feeling utterly old and weary, she walked into the mall before the gate sealed off the store, heading to the food court to get a small supper before going home to watch a holiday movie marathon on TNT. She was unprepared for the quiet,

"Nina James?" that greeted her as she passed the benches surrounding the fake jungle across from the anchor store.

She blinked. Ron Wright was standing in front of her. Mr. Handsome Corporate America in his suit and tie and perfect haircut had stood up to greet her, a small shopping bag in his hand.

"May I help you?" she asked automatically.

"Yes, you may," he replied in that same professional tone, though his eyes were twinkling. "I'm looking for a dinner partner for Christmas Eve. Will you join me?"

Nina's mind went blank. "For dinner?"

He nodded. "You're probably tired of eating at the food court. I think there's a restaurant upstairs."

"Sure." Still disbelieving, she followed him up the escalator to the restaurant on the second floor.

His eyes met hers as they seated themselves in one of the booths. "It's not as nice as the place we met before, but times are tough."

She murmured assent as the waiter arrived with glasses of water.

"I have a question for you," he said, peeling his straw and settling in his seat. "Why did you walk out on me that night?"

Nina felt the heat rise to her face. "You were obviously meeting someone else," she replied, not inclined to mentions her feelings of humiliation at being set up in the first place. "I didn't want to waste your time."

"You weren't wasting my time," he said quietly, "but it was getting hard to keep up the glad act. I didn't want to show up to a blind date with a pink slip in my hand, but I didn't want to stand you up, either. So," he spread his hands, "I tried to make the best of it."

Pink slip? "You got laid off?" she asked, staring at him.

"That very afternoon."

"But...but..." Nina groped for words. "I had no idea."

"It's not the sort of thing a guy wants to talk about on a first date. It doesn't exactly make a good impression."

"But you look so good..." Nina let her voice trail off. She hadn't meant to say it like that. She hadn't meant to say it at all.

"So do you." Ron smiled at her. "But unlike me, you don't have to keep up appearances with your family. I haven't told anyone that I'm out of work, except you and my sister."

"You're still out of work?"

His smile faded. "Yeah."

"I'm...I'm sorry," Nina faltered, cursing her own lack of tact. She sipped her water for composure. "Why are you telling me all this now?"

He gave her a serious look. "I haven't stopped thinking about you since that evening. I would have called you before, but most women don't want to waste their time with a brother without a job."

"What made you change your mind?"

"You have 'Spider Man 2' on DVD and I don't."

They both laughed, and Ron reached into his shopping bag and held out a box wrapped in gold and red Christmas paper. "This is for you."

Nina's breath caught in her throat. "For me?" She carefully tore the wrapping paper. Inside was the boxed fragrance set he'd bought from her a couple of weeks ago. She felt the blood rush to her stomach and raised her eyes to his, unable to speak for a moment.

"I guess you think I have a lot of nerve, coming on to a high-class woman like you with no job and no prospects," Ron began, still serious. "I won't be able to treat you the way you deserve and take you out a lot, but I would like to spend some time with you and get to know you better."

Talk about putting your pride in your pocket! Nina bit her lip, but a couple of tears straggled down her face anyway. She wiped them away and attempted a laugh.

"You were planning this when you bought this for me, weren't you?" she asked. "Trying to figure out what I like."

He shrugged. "I was thinking about it," he said. "I figured I could give it to my mother or my sister if I changed my mind."

"But you didn't change your mind."

"No."

"You must want to see my 'Spider Man 2' DVD bad," she remarked, folding up the wrapping paper.

"Does your system have Dolby?"

"And surround sound. But I was going to watch this holiday movie marathon on TNT."

"What? You can watch that tomorrow, it's going to run all day."

"Yeah, but if I let you watch 'Spider Man 2' on the second date, you won't have any reason to come back."

"Aw, come on, you know I'm not like that..."

Easter Weekend
By Maria Hogan Pereira

Good Friday

Good Friday always seemed such a stark, severe day. Mum would say it was a "deaf old day." In Ireland, we took the death of Jesus Christ very seriously. The pubs were shut for the whole day, as were all the shops. Christmas Day was the only other time that such a phenomenon occurred. And there were no newspapers on Good Friday. Everything closed for the day in memory of Jesus' suffering on the cross.

Daddy was completely off his routine, what with no newspaper and no pub. He used to have a few bottles of Guinness at home, but Irish men didn't like to drink at home in those days. He didn't complain, but there was a cheerless atmosphere about the house compounded by the simple dinner of fish and the church ceremonies that had to be attended. The services usually lasted at least two hours and were very hard on everybody. We had already spent two hours in the church on Holy Thursday, the day before, so we had had more than enough. My mother usually gave me some cleaning project on Good Friday, such as scouring the oven or sweeping under the beds, so that by day's end I had a sense of achievement. Daddy would catch up on some painting and dig his beloved garden in the evening.

Easter Saturday

After all the praying and deprivations of Good Friday, Easter Saturday was a great relief. It felt good to be back to our normal routine and have newspapers and pubs in our lives again. There was an underlying feeling of sadness that Jesus had been killed and the apostles were very depressed, but at least the agonies on the cross were dispensed with for another year.

There was also the serious business of Easter eggs to be considered. We did not have the tradition of painting real eggs as children in storybooks did. Our eggs came in boxes with shiny wrapping paper and gold and silver ribbons. Picked and reserved weeks in advance, they were brought home from the shop on Saturday and drooled over until Easter Day. Mum usually bought the eggs in Claire O'Boyle's sweet shop or Mattie Burns' Bus Stop. Otherwise it was a normal busy Saturday. Mum would go to Lipton's for the groceries and Clark's for the meat. Daddy went to Flanagan's for the coal and Dann's for the chicken and duck feed. There might be a trip to Johnson's for some clothes or Wood's for shoes.

Dinner on Saturday was always bacon and cabbage, but with spare ribs for me, as I couldn't stand the bacon and cabbage. None of us were ever made to eat anything we didn't like. The only thing forced on us was the spoonful of cod liver oil every night before bed. It was disgusting, tasting of fish and oil and probably liver, too, only I didn't know what that tasted like.

Easter Sunday

Finally Easter Sunday arrived. The sun shone, the air was crisp and we could feel spring. Everybody was up early and full of excitement. We had our boiled eggs and tea and toast. We put on our new Easter outfits with matching hats, piled into the car, and went to Mass. It was fairly elaborate but full of joy.

After Mass we came home and tuck into a breakfast cooked by Daddy. Doorsteps of toast and dollops of melting butter along with buckets of strong, sweet tea. Only after breakfast were we allowed to open our Easter eggs. We tried to devour them all at once but ended up nibbling all day.

Easter Sunday was truly a great day. We shook off the shackles of Lent and saw the weather turning. Dinner was the same as on St. Patrick's Day—roast lamb and vegetables, except that Mum sometimes made Baked Alaska as a special dessert for Easter. We usually didn't go anywhere on Easter Day, as staying at home with our eggs was good enough for us kids, and the grownups were probably tired from all the preparations.

Besides, we had to plan for Easter Monday. It was a bank holiday, and we would take a spin across the border to Enniskillen in Northern Ireland. It wrapped up the Holy Week with an exciting trip altogether.

Sweet Memories

Chocolate Easter bunnies, rock candy on a string, and Turkish taffy melting in the sun are sweet childhood memories. Baking cakes and brownies during my teen years filled my time and my hips. Middle age finds me in unknown territory, a victim of Syndrome X. A disorder that leaves me fuzzy-minded and tired, the result of eating too much comfort food. Each day is a struggle to find relief in lettuce and counting net carbs. I apply magnetic circles on pressure points to elevate my mood with the determination of a child peeling candy dots off paper strips.

—Lori Carruthers

Chapter 7

Falling In, Falling Out

Pergolesi
By Ellen Maidman-Tanner

> *Take the…willow winding paths*
> *Leading up and outward,*
> *This is what I give,*
> *This is what I ask you for;*
> *Nothing more.*
> —Judy Collins, "Since You Asked"

Bullshit. I ask for more! I asked for more and didn't get it, so I said, "So long for now." And bought myself a CD.

As the strains of Pergolesi's "Stabat Mater" poured through my ears and seeped into my soul, I realized I had bought the perfect farewell gift for myself to commemorate the two men I've loved. One had given me the appreciation for Baroque music, while the more recent of the two had given me big, macho speakers from which to listen to it. Both had many gifts to give. But both were incomplete, immature, "emotionally unavailable."

It appears I fall for brains, passion, and immaturity. Does maturity in men have to mean an absence of brains and passion? After a statistical base of two I am in no position to offer useful suggestions or direction one way or the other. I do, however, want to get this particular portion of my karma dry-cleaned soon and try to avoid falling into the same emotional bind. We go over our lessons until we get it right and can move on. I give heart and soul and get data and sex. And sometimes not enough of the latter.

Maybe I am barking up the wrong professions. One man was a scholar and university professor and one an environmental lawyer. I am thinking about taking a longer look at grease monkeys, accountants, and race car drivers. Maybe I am thinking about celibacy for a while. Maybe I don't know what to think.

How do I get the glory of passionate experience without the pain of departure? Maybe you can't have one without the other. It is an impressive process to live through. The sweet buildup of passion, the joy of emotional and physical connection, the unfolding of interests, habits, goals, and then the unraveling of the ties that bound.

Now that the kids are off in university, I must learn to deal with an existential self, if I can put aside the daily minutiae to realize that, for the first time in my life, I am further from a significant other than I've ever been. No intimate male. Just me.

And, despite the pain these two jerks inflicted, I miss them. I miss the look that, from time to time said, god-am-I-ever-happy-that-it-is-you-my-eyes-are-beholding-right-now. Sure, I can behold myself, but it's not the same. And yes, I know that I probably place too high a premium on male nurturing and attention dating back to some childhood experiences. Tough childhood experiences. Back then I learned to rely on my wit, speed, and creative ability.

Well, I still move quickly and my humor helps me glide at rapid surface speed, and I don't do art anymore and I still love myself. And respect myself. But each time some guy says, "Sorry, I can't be there for you," I hear, "not good enough, pretty enough, sexy enough, woman enough."

Enough.

So why does Collins' song keep tramping insistently through my brain? The words are poignant, poetic, and utterly unrealistic. Love 'em and merrily let 'em go somehow sounds like a balanced, rational, and cosmopolitan goal and one that, again, after achingly minor research, seems impossible to obtain. (What? No nightly call? No plans over the long weekend?)

I couldn't do it. I could not be a cool, aloof courtesan. I found myself diametrically opposed to this behavior. When I tried to be cool I ended up being too far away from who I truly am and from what I have to give anyone in the way of support, caring, and all-'round friendship. Take me, take my advice.

I stubbornly return to Pergolesi's ethereal harmonies, emitted by my massive new speakers, and they do soothe the

Insight

A woman friend had just introduced me to her male companion in a crowded bakery. His sapphire eyes fixed on me. A dazzling smile followed. During our small talk, those eyes never let mine go. I had never seen eyes so clear, so brilliant. No man had ever looked at me that intently, hanging on my every word. How embarrassing for our friend, a woman who might be romantically linked to him—I did not know for sure. As we parted ways among the jostling customers, I noticed what he was holding in his left hand. A white cane.

—Therese Keane

wounded yet hopeful heart. Gifts come in many strange and unpredictable packages. I optimistically adhere to the belief that there is still more good than bad in the balance.

It's definitely time to increase the statistical base. I think I like the notion of skipping from man to man like a series of rocks along the path of experience, frequently getting my feet soaked in between. Fortunately, I know enough math to have faith in demographics. My traits + life in Washington, D.C. = a good chance for positive outcome. In the meantime, I'll find different mirrors, different life stories, passions, and images of womankind held by new men, there for my reaping. And reap I shall.

Billy (fiction)
By Maria Hogan Pereira

Mary closed the door of Burke, Gilroy, Gannon and Co., Chartered Accountants, behind her and walked toward her Volkswagen Golf parked on Stephen Street. Thank God it was Friday. It would be good to get back home to Carrick on Shannon and see her mother.

As she drove toward the Dublin Road, she thought about the accountants' dinner dance that was coming up a week from now and there wasn't a sign of a man. What did she expect? There hadn't been a sign of a man since she had broken up with Sean Kelly from outside Mohill a year ago. It was still so hard to take the way he had dumped her for that nurse in Sligo General.

As she zigzagged over the Curlew Mountains she started to feel better. Something would turn up. Gosh, Sligo wasn't such a bad place, but there was no place like Carrick. She parked outside her mother's paper- and bookshop in Carrick on Shannon and went inside.

"Hello, love, how was the week in Sligo?" said her mother, Annie.

"Not too bad, Mum. How are tricks around here?"

"Grand, love."

"It's good to be home. Do you want me to take over here while you have your tea?"

"That would be great; I'm going to put on a fry. Oh, by the way, Nuala Donnelly phoned. She said she was thinking of going up to the rugby international in Dublin tomorrow and would you like to go?"

"Gosh, I'm desperate for a fellow for the accountants' 'do' next weekend."

"Oh yes! Right enough. It seems a shame to have to travel so far for a man, but you need your fun. You should go. Nell will be here to help me, so you're free as a bird."

Saturday morning saw Mary and Nuala heading up the Dublin Road in Nuala's Renault. They were a contrasting pair: Mary tall and thin with dark straight hair, and Nuala small and blonde and not quite so thin. They didn't have tickets for the match, but that didn't bother them. They would head for some of the pubs near Lansdowne Road and watch it on the telly. It would be just as good. Actually, thought Mary, it might be better, being fond of her comfort.

It was a nice crisp morning and as Mary looked at the fields of sheep and cows go by, she felt glad to be heading to the city. God knows whom they'd meet. Rugby players were often good-looking and usually came from respectable families.

By the time they hit the outskirts of Dublin it was noon and they were feeling peckish.

"Let's go over to Donnybrook, dump the car, and get some grub in Eddie Rocket's," said Nuala. "I love that American food."

As they munched their BLTs in Eddie Rocket's, they watched the scores of Irish rugby fans walking by in their green and white colors. There were the Welsh in their red and white.

"I'd love to meet a Welsh bloke," said Mary.

"What good would he be living in Cardiff or somewhere? Besides, you need a local for your dinner dance," Nuala replied.

"Oh, I'd just love to hear him talk," said Mary.

"Talk?" said Nuala. "I thought all they were good for was singing."

They walked a few streets and into McDaid's pub. It was crowded but they found a table and ordered two pints of Smithwicks. There they sat surrounded by roaring drunken rugby fans. There they sat ignored by these same roaring drunks. Mary had one more pint and was beginning to roar herself. It was the best of fun. Rugby was a powerful game altogether.

As Mary, on her fourth pint, stood up to cheer for the great goal shot by the Irish team, she met Billy. He had been standing beside her for quite a while. He said it was a great match. Mary agreed. He asked her would she like a drink. Mary took a quick look. He was a decent height with an okay face. Small, slightly slit eyes, but a very nice layered haircut that suited him very well. He looked well dressed in his sweater and jeans. Not too bad.

They chatted amiably, and when Nuala finally dragged her out of the pub the deal was done. Billy had said he'd be delighted to come to Carrick on Shannon the following weekend.

Mary picked Billy up at the train and they drove back to her mother's shop. Billy was wearing a nice brown coat with what looked like a very decent suit underneath. No problem there. Sometimes men could be lousy dressers.

Billy proudly handed Mary a box of chocolates. He chatted happily about his father and brother, who were big rugby fans. He worked in his dad's business in Dublin, which he enjoyed. Mary couldn't quite fathom his looks. She wasn't attracted to him, but for an escort to a dinner dance that wasn't a prerequisite. No, there was something unusual about his features, but no matter; time to have a quick bite at home and get ready for the dance.

Mary and Billy ate Annie's delicious salad sandwiches with cups of tea. Billy sat watching TV, which he said he loved. Mary went upstairs to the bedroom to put on her beautiful white halter-neck dress. She just loved that dress. It felt so good to be getting dressed up for a change. So what if she wasn't mad about Billy, at least people would see that she could get herself a man, even after Sean Kelly.

Then it happened. The bomb was dropped. Annie came into the room and asked Mary did she realize that Billy was "slightly different." What was wrong with her? Couldn't she have seen that before she dragged the poor fellow down here? Mary went rigid with shock. It couldn't be true, but even as she thought it, everything clicked into place. Of course that was the thing she couldn't quite put her finger on. Billy's features had that tell-tale look. His conversation was stilted and had a lot of key words in it like "magic" and "super." But lots of Dubliners used these words. They were "in" words, though Mary wouldn't have used them herself.

Oh God, what was she going to do? If Mum had picked up on Billy's handicap so fast, so would everybody at the accountants' dance. No point in presuming that they were all as blind as she. Oh God! Oh God! What was she going to do? But wait a minute. Nuala hadn't noticed, either, and Nuala hadn't been drinking much because she had been driving. Besides, she was dressed and ready to go and so was Billy.

"Well, Mum I'll have to just brazen it out. All of them are going to think I was really desperate, and they are right. But so what? It's too late to back out now."

Mary and Billy went to the dance. Mary wondered how she had missed his complete lack of succinct conversation. Probably because she talked so much herself. It was no wonder she was 25 and manless. Who could ever want her?

They entered the ballroom of the Bush Hotel and Mary introduced Billy to everybody, looking at them sideways to see did they notice anything. She started to count the times Billy said "magic" and "super." Far too many. The potatoes were super and so were the carrots and brussels sprouts. It started to grate on her nerves. She couldn't think of anything to say to Billy. As the night wore on she started to talk to other people and Billy, feeling lost, started to resort to his key phrases more and more. The bubble was really burst.

The next morning she drove Billy to the train first thing. "I thought I was staying for the weekend in the country," he protested. Mary told him firmly that he would have been but her Aunt Philomena had suddenly gotten sick. Mary and her mother would have to visit her right away in Ballinamore. Billy still protested, but Mary said no. He'd be bored to tears hanging around all day in her aunt's house. Billy boarded the train totally dejected. Mary heaved a sigh of relief. Those rugby matches weren't all they were cracked up to be.

Ten years later, John O'Connell came cruising down the Shannon with some friends. He was an American lawyer whose parents had come from Aughavas. He came wandering into Annie's shop, where Mary was unloading some books. He was looking for some poems by Yeats and Mary sold him a book by Dermot Healy. John was impressed. They married and Mary moved to America.

The following year Mary lay on her hospital bed cradling her beautiful newborn son. She was trying to come to terms with what the doctor had just told her. Kieran had Down syndrome.

She tried to think through the dark and bottomless place where her mind was meant to be. She played with his fingers and marveled at how she loved this little boy so much and she thought, not of Billy, but of Billy's mother. How she must have worried as he set off on that train with his box of chocolates to meet a young woman, but she let him go. How well she had reared him. Billy's self-esteem was higher than Mary's at that time. Then what comfort she must have had to offer when the rejected Billy came home a day early on a flimsy excuse. What a great woman she was. What a great mother!

The Sorrow of Small Losses
By Deborah Hefferon

The second hand fell off of my alarm clock sometime last Monday. The red wand that ticked like a heartbeat simply slid down to the bottom of the black cube that jolts me out of my deep sleep on weekdays. It's just lying there behind the plastic face cover under the 6. I was accustomed to the white noise of the soft ticking. It reassured me, although I didn't appreciate that reassurance until it was gone. Now I have to stare at the silent clock to see if the batteries are still working. The sweep of the black minute hand past a minute or two doesn't cause much of a stir—I can easily miss it. My mornings are different now. There is a void where the blocks of 60 seconds of ticking used to be.

*   *   *

A friend whom I hadn't seen for 16 years was in town last Thursday. I made dinner for him and we caught up on each other's lives. I should explain that I had seen him only once before in my life. I met him when I was disembarking from a flight to Lisbon on a gray Thanksgiving morning. He asked me if I could recommend a hotel, which I did, and we shared a taxi to the *pension* in Lisbon's lower town. He was en route to a medical conference in Rome and had scheduled 24 hours to play in Lisbon, a new city for him. I found myself in the city because I had won a free ticket from a TWA contest. My good fortune was somewhat diminished by my inability to take leave from my counseling job. The four-day holiday weekend afforded me the chance to compromise—a few decadent days for Christmas shopping in Portugal.

We spent the day together and it was an unexpectedly glorious union of souls: he, a rational scientist, and I, a bleeding-heart type. We found obvious delight in discovering the old quarter of Lisbon and in each other. After walking around the hilly city, visiting the coach museum and paying homage to the Christopher Columbus monument, we sought out a typical Portuguese restaurant to hear singers of *fado*, ballads of loss and longing. We drank Mateus wine and listened to the melancholy songs. Around us the local diners wiped their teary eyes and raised their glasses during the refrains. For us, the evening was funny and tender and a little sad.

When we got back to the hotel, we stood in the doorway, under a candlelit statue of the Blessed Virgin. We were slightly drunk and giggly and the romance of the intimate and labyrinthine cobblestone alleyways and the haunting *fado* caught up with us: Leaning against the stone wall, we kissed. I remember hearing and feeling our hearts beating. I remember the rough wall behind my head. Both of us were married and I felt naughty and alarmed at this moment; I was sure he did, too. We went to our separate rooms and the next morning while I slept off the wine, he flew off to present his conference paper. I spent the remainder of the weekend shopping for pottery and ceramic tiles.

We've kept in touch sporadically over the years and, now and then, we have mutually expressed that meeting each other was a significant gift. We talked about many things when we got together the other night, including that day we met. He remembered parts of the day I had forgotten: specifics of what we had spoken about (dreams) and what we had eaten (cubes of pork braised with baby clams still in the shell); I recalled the walk home (we missed the last clanging streetcar and walked home in the rain from the *fado* club). Reconstructing our conversation reminded me of two split halves of a pendant heart that neatly fit together.

When he was leaving my house the other night, he kissed me good-night very sweetly and said, "That's the kiss we never had and that I've always wished we *had* had."

"What about those kisses in the doorway of the *pension*?" I asked.

"I don't remember that we kissed."

Thud. A memory drops off the edge of the earth. Although I hadn't consciously thought about those kisses for the 16 years that separated us from our first meeting, their loss made me feel like a widow.

*   *   *

Last week the comforting ticking of a red second hand and the memory of kisses were snatched away. Now there is an empty space, like heartache, waiting to be filled.

Chapter 8

Beyond the Garden Wall

The Memory of Sound
By Deborah Hefferon

I have traveled to many places, but last month, in West Africa, in a game park where the jungle meets the savanna, I heard a way to my past. On that day, two companions and I picnicked on our driver's straw prayer mat by the river. We chose the spot because we could keep an eye out for bathing hippos while we ate our French bread sandwiches. Around our picnic spot, the ground was littered with fallen fronds, bleached pale gray by the African sun, like driftwood on a deserted beach. The grass beneath us was high and dry and prickly. Our mat refused to lie earth-flat; we pushed it down with slaps of open hands, but it floated up like a hovercraft. We three sat in defiance, spreading out our plates and food and bottled water—but, between the plastic food containers and our legs, the mat swelled in waves.

As though it were a premonition, I felt seasick. And then, so far inland, I heard the ocean. I peered through the grasses at the placid, brown river. Not a ripple, yet I *heard* the ocean. Looking skyward, I saw the dried fronds of a thick-trunked palm tree caught in a small whirlwind: they crackled and heaved, mimicking waves crashing.

I closed my eyes and found myself in the tiny guesthouse in Candidesa in Bali, where years ago, the thunderous ocean waves crashing against the sea wall one night had kept me awake. My ears had echoed for days afterward—my head had become a conch shell. Now I sat beneath a palm tree in West Africa and recaptured the sticky, sleepless night in Bali; I heard those waves again.

As though some hole had been pierced in my audio memory, sounds from the past started to stream through into my consciousness. Sounds made significant by their clarity came to life through their very ability to transcend the world's din. Long after my friends and the driver had walked to the river's edge and called to me, "Debbie, come here! Water buffalo in a mud puddle!" I continued to sit on that straw mat, while memories of sounds began to parade through the speakers in my mind and my heart.

Smells and sights and touch arrive in my mind with such a rush of familiarity that I take it for granted *they* can be reclaimed—the scent of cinnamon and apples and I see my mother sliding a pie out of the white enamel oven; a profile glimpsed in the midst of heavy traffic is a cameo of my grandmother; a velvety blanket that my finger skims on a department store shelf triggers a worn one that I clenched when I was sick at age 5.

Certainly there are sounds, born in my childhood and recalled throughout my adult years, that have continued to soothe—steady, rhythmic rain hitting the ground, skimming the window, bouncing off a tin roof; or a screen door slamming, evoking summer freedom. But compared to the memories of my other senses, I might as well have been deaf. Now, the intensity of my sound memories startles me.

Click-clack, click-clack. Feet running up the cement stairwell in my apartment building, heels smacking across the Metro platform, even occasionally the clip-clop of a policeman on horseback, summon an image of my mother's spike-heeled shoes.

It is the summer my mother and I move into my grandmother's house, after my parents' divorce. My mother has a job as a salesgirl and dresses up every day. Out of the tissue paper, from the shoeboxes jammed into the narrow closet in the back bedroom, come high heels: black patent leather, white lizard skin, and strappy, shiny, red shoes. The heels are so slim that when we go to the Atlantic City boardwalk, my mother has to buy special rubber tips to push on the ends of the heels so that she won't get stuck between the wooden planks. At 9, I find this very sophisticated, very much the image I want to own when I grow up. Click-clack. My mother walks up the front steps of the house, across the tiled vestibule, and up the wooden staircase to our bedroom, where I pretend to be sleeping.

A thud in the distance. I hear the whack of a tennis ball and I travel back 10 years to an excursion my husband and I took in Iraq, near the Syrian border.

It is early morning and we are waiting for our host to escort us to an archeological site. I sit outside the housing compound on a low stone wall. Cement buildings rise behind me; in the foreground are piles of rubble seen through the wavy heat; and beyond, the sand that obeys no political borders. There is absolute stillness and silence except for a small whirlpool of sand blowing around my feet and the sound of tennis balls—back and forth, back and forth—regular, steady, like the beating of a heart, off in the distance. An auditory mirage perhaps, but a sound that surrounds me and burrows in my memory. It is somehow the clearest, most distinct sound that I have ever heard, so real that I can retrieve it at will.

Last year, a friend gave me a necklace for my birthday; at the end of its long, delicate chain hangs a small silver globe with the earth's land masses carved in brass. Inside is a tiny chime that can be heard only when the world is very, very quiet. I wore the necklace several times before I realized the faint chiming was coming from my own chest. Hearing it gives me a simple joy because I know it is a special moment when I can be aware of such stillness. I believe that recognizing how precious it is to hear this secret chime and to know how rare are the pockets of silence in my life was the beginning. It awakened my mind's ear, and the ocean came to me in the jungle.

The Water
By Caroline Cottom

First graceful and soft, a shower;
then the immutable Fijian sky
dumps on us in surprise
so thick that we've lost the harbour.

Umbrellas burst and wither,
sidewalks swim under water.
The rain sloughs down invisible spouts
and slinks like a snake around corners.

Inked with rain,
everyone slips in after lunch
brown faces streaming
shirts dark and clinging;

my blue sandals have spread
on my soles as though I've walked in ink,
could stamp the floor
with my tremulous Caucasian feet.

Already I've forgotten driving
on the right, the snap of broccoli
stalks, "harbor" for "harbour"—
will I find my way home?

My blue pen leaks as I write;
the inky deep of the Pacific
finds the whorls of my fingers,
makes mystic signs on my palm.

Walking on the Moon
By Julia Weller

In my closet, I keep an old jewelry box that I take out on rainy summer days when our community pool is closed and my youngest daughter, Daisy, is bored. We sit on the bed and tip out the contents—charm bracelets that my sister and I wore as children, a silver compact inlaid with a portrait of a bewigged lady that belonged to my Russian godmother, broken necklaces, single earrings, a filigree cigarette holder that my mother used in the days when she smoked, and tiny pieces of twisted driftwood picked up on long-forgotten holidays. Daisy loves to sort through the pile and to try on the jewelry that isn't broken.

"When did you get this, Mummy?" she asked recently. She twisted the large, tarnished ring embossed with a geometric design around her slender finger.

"It was the day that the first man landed on the moon," I said. "A long time ago."

Ocean Sky

Bits of blue paper
flutter from the roof, broken
pieces of the sky.

Five black metal birds
shatter the silent shoreline,
whirling against wind.

Colors of striped sky
languish inside a sunset
burning the last light.

The moon's grizzled face
in a velvet night painting
caught Francis Bacon.

—Therese Keane

I was traveling through Europe with Joan, a college classmate, and her cousin Ron, a tall, humorless engineering student. We had taken the boat at daybreak from Piraeus to one of the many Greek islands scattered in the Aegean Sea. The village was on the top of a steep slope and the road up to the village circled round and round. We passed tiny whitewashed houses bejeweled with crimson and purple flowers. A little girl leading a donkey smiled shyly at us. In the dusty square, we saw a café with tables and chairs under umbrellas.

"Great," said Joan. "Let's get some breakfast, I'm starved."

The woman behind the counter spoke almost no English but seemed to understand us when we asked her if there were any rooms to rent in the village. She shook her head, which we knew meant "yes," not "no," and pointed to herself. Stepping out of the gloom into the brilliant sunshine, she called out a name and the little girl we had seen with the donkey came running. After we had eaten a plentiful meal of crisp brown bread, feta cheese, ripe tomatoes, and delicious black olives, the child led us further up the mountain to a flat-topped house with an outside staircase that led to a little room on the roof. This was to be our home for the next few days. It was only after she had left that I noticed there was no lock on the door. I pointed it out to Joan but she laughed off my concern. She had a socialist's blind faith in the innate goodness of everyone who lived in a less developed economy.

"Besides," she said cheerily, "Ron is here too." I didn't share her confidence in the dour Ron's sense of chivalry or the purity of the intentions of some of the men we had seen lounging outside the tavern in the village. Their welcoming smiles had more closely resembled leers and I became uncomfortably aware of the shortness of my miniskirt when compared to the long dark dresses worn by most of the women we had seen. It had also struck me that we were the only tourists to have disembarked from the ferry. This island was obviously not a tourist hot spot.

Ron was less concerned about the missing lock than about finding a television somewhere on the island so we could watch the moon landing we had heard about on the ferry. Back at the café that night, we were able to make our landlady understand what we wanted and she pointed across the street to the *kaphenia*, the tavern. It was traditionally a place for men only, but Joan had no hesitation in breaching the male sanctuary. I felt distinctly uneasy as we entered the dark, smoky room. We were the only women but no one seemed to notice us. Everyone was crowded around the black and white TV on the bar, watching the blurry figure of Neil Armstrong taking his first steps across the moon's surface. We joined them and listened to the voices we could not understand explaining the pictures on the screen.

When it was over, the TV was turned off and our presence suddenly became the topic of conversation. We were motioned to seats around a table, next to some older men. The younger men sat at a different table. The radio had been turned on at a deafening volume and the center of the room was cleared. A few men got up and began to dance with their arms on each other's shoulders. A stringed instrument was brought out and the owner struck up a plaintive tune out of time to the song on the radio. The dancers shuffled back and forth in the haze of smoke. Joan began clapping her hands wildly. We had been drinking retsina, the harsh Greek wine that smelled like something meant for cleaning floors, and were now on to ouzo, an even stronger liquor, ordered by the old man with the bristling handlebar mustache sitting next to me. Suddenly Joan grabbed Ron's hand and dragged him, protesting, out onto the dance floor.

"You're making a fool of yourself!" he hissed through clenched teeth. Joan ignored him and the dancers broke formation to make room for them in the line. The alcohol was beginning to have an effect on me and I felt pleasantly drowsy. When my gray-haired drinking companion suddenly stood up, bowed stiffly to me, and offered his arm, I happily joined in. Ron and I towered over the Greeks and they had to raise their arms above their shoulders to hang on to us. But they didn't seem to mind. They carried us with them back and forth across the dance floor in time to the twanging rhythms from the musician in the corner, now no longer competing with the radio. The old men moved with surprising agility and praised us with their eyes as we caught on to the twisting and turning dance steps, crossing one foot in front of the other. The piquant scent of the *tsatsiki,* the circle of happy glowing faces, and the Greek music pouring into the hot night air dissolved any sense of strangeness. When at last the dancing stopped and we all sank back exhausted onto our chairs, even Ron was smiling.

The old man who had asked me to dance reached into his pocket and, taking my hand, pressed something into my palm. In the dim light I could make out the shape of a ring. He gave me a wide, gap-toothed grin. Befuddled with ouzo and exertion, I wondered if he were proposing marriage. Then he raised his tumbler and said something about *Ellas America,* so I knew he was drinking to friendship between his rocky home and the country that had put a man on the moon.

"Efharisto," I said, raising my tumbler in response. "Thank you."

I slid the ring over my finger. It was much too big but I held my hand up to show him I was wearing it.

When Joan and I stood up to leave, my grizzled companion took my hand and, bending his head, kissed it. "Thank you," I said again. Ron had not stirred. "Aren't you coming?" Joan asked. "Not yet," her cousin answered. His voice was slurred and he was half lying, half sitting in his chair. We shrugged and left him there.

Outside, the moon was a perfect white hole cut out of an inky paper sky. Joan and I walked a little way up the hill out of the village and then stopped, gazing up at the moon. We couldn't see them, yet we knew that there were human beings up there. Something of mystery had been lost: The moon was no longer Diana the huntress, the goddess riding the night sky. It had been reduced to a pockmarked rock, conquered and knowable, just like the one we were standing on. I felt sad that another frontier had been breached.

Then we heard footsteps coming up behind us, and we made out the figures of two young men from the *kaphenia.* They were drunk, laughing and shouting. They had obviously followed us and called out to us in Greek.

"C'mon!" Joan grabbed my arm. "Let's go!"

There was no one else on the road. We ran and they ran after us. Panting, we dashed up the stairs to our room and it was then I remembered there was no lock. Frantically, I looked about for something to wedge against the door, but there was no time. We leaned against it with all our weight as they shoved from the outside, trying to push it open.

"Go away!" I shouted. "Leave us alone!" I hoped that my yelling might waken our landlady down below, but their laughter drowned me out.

The door gave a little and one of them put his hand through the crack. *"Amerikani! Amerikani!"* they taunted us. "I'm not American!" Joan shouted irrelevantly. She was a fierce Canadian nationalist, but I doubted that carried any weight with the Greeks outside. Instead, I gave a sharp thrust to the door and heard the satisfying crunch of the invader's hand being squashed against the frame. He cried out in pain, and I released my weight just enough to let him remove his hand. I was angry that these boors had shattered the feeling of kinship I'd felt at the tavern and didn't care if he was hurt. It didn't occur to me that they might have misinterpreted our entry into their male sanctum.

A few minutes later we heard their ignominious retreat down the staircase. Joan and I grinned victoriously at each other. Ron's arrival a short while later probably had more to do with the departure of the two men than our show of force. At 6 feet 2 inches, he was a head taller than all the dancers at the kaphenia. But he seemed not to have noticed anyone coming down the stairs and made no reply when we asked him. Instead, he fell straight onto his bed in the corner, his feet dangling off the end, and began snoring loudly. Joan and I giggled hysterically, as much in relief as at Ron. But we dragged the dresser up against the door anyway.

The next morning, I found the ring on the floor by my bed.

"Can I have it, Mummy, please? Look, the silver is coming off. You won't wear it any more." Actually, I've never worn it. But I did keep it.

I shake my head. "No," I say. "It's a souvenir from the night the moon was conquered. An old Greek fisherman gave it to me. I wouldn't want to lose it now."

Unfamiliar Territory
By Deborah Hefferon

My friend, Melanie, has asked me to talk to her daughter, Nora, who is about to go to West Africa as a Peace Corps volunteer. Melanie thinks that, because I was a volunteer 22 years ago on the same continent, I will have wise counsel to share, words that will illuminate and protect.

I don't know Nora very well. We have sat at the same table celebrating holidays and birthdays a few times over the years. I know about her from stories that her mother has shared with me; she knows me from anecdotes about my world travels that I've recited in her presence. Melanie has told me that Nora thinks I'm really funny. This seems to be important to Melanie because she worries that Nora, now in her mid-20s, doesn't have enough of a sense of humor. I try to remember ever having had a personal conversation with Nora before. I recall that one time she phoned me for advice about university admissions, but I suspect that was as a result of her mother's urging. She listened politely but I doubt that she followed my advice.

I have a hunch that Melanie had to talk Nora into this chat also, but she arrives at my apartment promptly at four. She is still the sober young woman I last saw a year ago at a family picnic—tight, straight-legged jeans, no makeup, long, straight blonde hair that she fingers from time to time. We talk about her work as an RN with AIDS patients and her need to see another side of life, which travel and the Peace Corps offer.

I serve tea and chocolate-covered fortune cookies. I think that the cookies will be a good icebreaker, a safety net, just in case we don't have much to say to each other. But we do. We talk for a long time, until the sun goes down, until we are sitting in dusk. We speak of practical things: the shots to get, how often I was able to get together with the other volunteers, what language training was like. We speak of emotions: the excitement of change, the anticipation of self-discovery, the sadness of leaving friends and family behind, the fear of isolation, the thrill of traveling to new places. She asks me about all the places I lived and traveled before I was married.

"Haven't you ever been scared?" she asks earnestly. She admits to me that she has been afraid since she heard about that Fulbright scholar who was murdered in South Africa a few months ago. She says that the closer she gets to the date of departure, the more she realizes what a safe life she has led so far. Even though she works with the dying, she has foolishly trusted in a belief that she will always be safe.

"One of the things I like most about myself is that I'm open. Open to new adventures and cultures and people. But how can I protect myself? The world is a scarier place now than when you were in the Peace Corps."

*   *   *

"Poems written in Arabic can't be translated into English without losing their soul. Listen, just listen to the beauty unfold."

I listened. At first my tired mind, clouded by the late hour and the Beaujolais, struggled to grasp the few words and phrases I understood in classical Arabic, and then I surrendered. I allowed the beauty to unfold. Trusting in the melody that cloaked me, I felt the earth move.

"That was beautiful."

"That last one, I wrote. Come. I will show you more at my house," whispered the poet in his silky-accented voice. He rose in a fluid movement from the chair. His smooth face and his lean body were that of a boy's—it was hard to believe that words of such wisdom and insight could have come from the person who stood before me.

*   *   *

It was my season of superlatives, as I referred to it in my journal at the time. Without years and seasoning for comparison, I somehow felt confident that I was at my emotional and spiritual height: my most confident, my most liberated, my most giving and receptive. My karma was so good. I was constantly in motion: quaking with idealism, seeking truth, stretching. Everything beckoned to me then. I was a sage inviting new experiences that would enhance me and clarify the mysteries. It almost breaks my heart to reach back in my mind's files to recall how acutely conscious I was of being on the threshold of life—and how trusting I was. I didn't know then that life can be a trickster.

*   *   *

I had entered the Peace Corps fresh out of college and was assigned to Tangier, but that weekend, I was visiting my friend Carole in Marrakesh. I met the poet at a party that was crammed with other volunteers and Moroccans. A party at which, Carole promised, I would get to know the real Morocco. I was leaving with the poet when Carole warned, "Debbie, you don't know this guy."

"Oh, Carole," I smiled, as I took his hand.

We crossed the vast Jemaa el-Fna Square, usually a sideshow of bustling energy. It was empty but just that morning, Carole and I had spent time in the square bargaining with the itinerant vendors who offered shiny silver jewelry, popcorn, wooden spoons, hashish pipes, and Koranic texts. We took photos of

From a Trip to Egypt

We visit the tombs in the Valley of Kings. It is 110 degrees outside. A tourist from Oman invites us to visit his country, but confesses it gets even hotter there. The heat is oven-like, while the tombs are cool. I joke with Michael that if I had been a scribe in Pharaonic Egypt, I'd continually invent more history to write in tinier and tinier glyphs, just so that I could stay cool underground. ("But, Your Highness, what about the battles of your great-uncle once removed? Surely we must record these great events....")

I overhear an elderly Chinese-American tourist mutter, "There is nothing new under the sun." Catching up with him outside the tomb, I ask what he meant. He tells me that in China there is a saying, "When the Emperors build tombs, the city weeps." This refers to the Chinese royal practice of killing and entombing those who have built the tombs. As in China, so in ancient Egypt.

—Ellen Maidman-Tanner

performing acrobats encircled by gawking tourists and small laughing boys. We bought brochettes from an elderly robed man who squatted by his little charcoal stove fanning the skewers of meat. He complimented us when we spoke to him in Arabic. After a siesta on Carole's rooftop, we had returned to the square to watch the late afternoon unfold in its pageantry of snake charmers, dancers, musicians, sword-swallowers, fire-eaters, and storytellers. The absence of activity—except for a few men seated in the flickering light of their gas lamps, drinking tea and smoking their water pipes—was striking. The square was mine. I spun around, heady with the exotic stillness and the orange-blossom-scented air. The silhouetted Koutoubia tower, minarets crowned with light, and the Atlas Mountains flashed by my eyes as I whirled with my arms extended. The poet laughed at my spontaneous dance, my joy—my joy seemed infectious.

We walked through the massive stone gate and entered the souk with its shops' heavy wooden shutters latched. Moonglow, seeping romantically through the canvas-draped ceilings and wooden slats, and the occasional bare light bulb lit the way.

Then we filtered into the bowels of the medina, where the darkness was deep. I tripped over a stone and felt unsure if I should continue, but at that very moment the poet took my hand. He guided me through the mystical labyrinth of narrow paths, past shuttered stalls and terracotta houses. We took a sharp turn into a smaller alley and climbed rickety wooden steps that delivered us to a large room, opening onto a balcony. Nearby a baby cried and voices whispered; doves cooed in the rafters. He put his hands on my shoulders and gently pushed me down on a low banquette. I whispered, "Please put a light on so we can read your poetry." My heart thumped for all the world to hear.

He laughed softly. "That's not why we're here."

The night sounds stopped abruptly, *or did I just stop hearing them?* as he sat down beside me, hip to hip, shoulder to shoulder, and turned to me. His sour breath coated me as he grabbed me and pushed me onto my back. My head hit a metal edge. Dazed, my eyes roamed and fell on a candle glimmering in the corner. Had it been there when we entered?

"I'm not here," I said to myself. But I couldn't convince myself because his mouth assaulted my lips. His spiny tongue invaded my mouth. *I wonder now, why did I part my lips?* His rough hands fumbled around my neck. *Where were my hands?* He ripped open my blouse. "What are you doing?" I whispered. *Why didn't I yell?* He bit my nipples. He cursed my jeans as he pulled at my crotch. I undid the snaps and the buttons and the zipper. *How could I have helped him?* My eyes frantically sought the candle, but it was gone. The loss left me saturated with sadness. I sobbed silently, trying to emit sounds that crouched in my throat. I was choking. He forced his penis into my mouth. I gagged. My own hands rose to my throat and pushed him away. He released me for a second, and then I felt cold, sharp metal at my chin. Again and again, I repeated my mantra: "This is not happening to me." I sucked in my breath as he drove his penis into my pants, into me, and quickly, it was over. He rolled off me, onto the floor. The knife lay by my head; I didn't dare move. There was darkness and stillness and my nothingness.

Time passed. *How much time? Two minutes or an hour, I honestly don't know.* I got up at a sleepwalker's pace. I zipped my pants, hooked my bra, buttoned my blouse, found my purse. My eyes adjusted to the blackness until I could make out the doorway hung with cloth.

As though we were two acquaintances who had just shared a cup of tea, he said, "You can't find your way back to the square. I will take you."

He stood up, wrapped a burnoose around himself, and pushed me gently through the door. I stumbled on the stairs and he steadied me. A large woman was sitting on the bottom step nursing a baby. Her head was bowed as if in prayer.

I followed a few steps behind him through the claustrophobic tunnel of the alley, the medina, the souk. I kept my eyes straight ahead until they beheld a taxi parked at the edge of the square. Lit from within, it was like a mirage that any moment could be snuffed out. Then the poet turned back, passing me in silence, and I walked toward the taxi. The rear door opened for me.

*   *   *

I want to say something meaningful, something helpful to Nora. I say that it's wise of her to be concerned with her safety and that we all need to balance our openness with an awareness of reality. I suspect that she wants a more solid answer than this. I tell her that I have recently reread the journal that I kept when I was a volunteer. In a bold move that alarms me, I ask her if she might like to read it, but I warn her, there were times when I wasn't so safe, I wasn't so happy. I can tell she's surprised, perhaps embarrassed by my offer.

"No, thanks anyway. Really, sometime I'd love to read it but I have so little time left and I have so much to read anyway, about Cameroon and all, and I need to brush up on my French. So much to do before I leave, ya know?"

I am filled with my shame of silence and unspoken warnings as I watch her gather up her purse and bags. I realize that we haven't touched the cookies. In answer to her question about self-protection, I give her amulets—three fortune cookies—which I place carefully in her jacket pocket. She gives me a peck on the cheek and I demonstrate how the French double kiss.

Salvador

Maria says to me, "Look. Don't turn your eyes.
Lupe is dead by their hands."
I think the world will break under my gaze
and the photograph utter a cry. Here is
Lupe's face, white with the silence of egrets;
Maria and her mother in shadow, as though
I have entered a grotto. I lower my eyes:
Maria's hands are feathers that Lupe's face
spreads into wings. Her mother's are
knots of roots, taut with determination.
Between them, they anchor Lupe's life
and let it turn to the sky.

—Caroline Cottom

I open the front door of my apartment. The hallway is brightly lit. In the artificial light, she looks so young, going out into the clearing of life.

Chapter 9

Where We've Been

The Fields at Arles
By Caroline Cottom

Sunflowers sway as if to music. Ocher medallions sing vibrantly, full of light. Brassy yellows, the hallmark of Vincent van Gogh's stay in southern France, appear in his paintings as café lights, wheat fields, the sun of Arles—his "high yellow note."

For many years, van Gogh represented a fountain of creative energy that was for me both a blessing and a curse. His brush strokes and wild torrents of color captivated me. Yet if I'd written his epitaph, it would read, "Brilliant and prolific, he created himself to death." Somewhat like my father.

When I was 12, my father came home with easels, brushes, and a set of Winsor-Newton oils and announced that he was taking my sister and me into the hills above San Clemente. It was summer, the tall grasses of Southern California as golden as wheat, and below us the red-tiled roofs of stucco houses—white and aqua and buff—spread out like a fan. Beyond stretched a tawny beach and water like indigo ink.

My father, excited by the task, framed a scene with his hands, coaxing us to do the same. Cathy and I made windows with our fingers and thumbs, then watched as he sketched with a dark pencil on crisp white canvas. Our own lines were more tentative, but we grew bold as we mixed the blues—cobalt and aquamarine—on a white paper palette, later adding titanium white, crimson, and black. The top of the sky would be vivid, then soften toward the horizon, graying and muting until the blue was almost gone, as though carried on the wind to China. By the end of the day, we had smeared the palette with every color: lemon yellow, cadmium orange, burnt sienna, raw umber, chromium green. Painting with my father and sister was the richest creative experience I'd ever had, and I was grateful for the lessons.

Painting was a side interest in my father's turbulent life. While I was growing up, he was a traveling salesman, gone for months at a time. He tried setting up businesses at home—a print shop, a woodworking operation, a clothes-hamper factory—not wanting to travel but invariably ending up back on the road. Later, when he was able to stop traveling, he designed and built automated machines, then restored antique furniture and fine china.

All of this my father did with great creative energy and uncurbed feeling.

Often overrun by emotion, he was like a 2-year-old raging and storming, out of control. In the midst of a project, his frustration at fever pitch, he would kick the tires of his Cadillac or punch his fist through the kitchen wall.

In my mind, the two went together—my father's surges of creativity and his fury. Both seemed to well up from the same deep cauldron. I tried to stay away from his outbursts, which intimidated and frightened me. Because of his rages, I became afraid of my own highs and lows, which coursed through me like the California tides.

> Fall
>
> Greeted by a world
> cloaked in full fall raiment
> We see how much
> we will never know
>
> The golden carpet of leaves
> floats out beneath our feet
> It is sunlight brought to rest
>
> in the dreamy collapse
> of the chilled afternoon
> Bare branches reach out whispering of time
>
> Molecule to molecule
> Dust to dust
>
> Winter will envelop all soon.
>
> —Ellen Maidman-Tanner

I was relieved when I could finally leave home. Because I'd showed talent in math, I studied calculus and Russian my freshman year; then I transferred, for financial reasons, to a school closer to home, where there was no Russian and a poor math department. Searching for a new direction, I fell in love with English literature and changed fields completely, to major in literature and art.

When I wasn't reading Dickens or writing poetry, I drew and painted. The largest of my efforts, a five-by six-foot acrylic, was a figure seated on a bench, bent over in resignation. At the college art show, "Woman in Blue and Green" caught the eye of a professor, who bought it for her living room. I was thrilled, as I'd never dreamed my art would sell. That same year, I had some poems and stories published in the school's literary journal, but I discounted that accomplishment because it was merely a college publication.

It didn't occur to me that I could fare better than my father, whose artistic genius was never rewarded. Over the years I had watched him lurch from project to project, making money and losing it on one creative scheme after another.

But even van Gogh was not recognized for his art during his lifetime; he sold only one painting publicly. In "Night Café," he painted in deep yellow, red, and green. Lamps vibrating against the dark red wall, a man beside a pool table who stares warily out. Vincent wrote that he wanted to depict a place where one's emotions could run wild, where a man might commit murder. Although the critics rejected his bold strokes of color—indeed, only one praised his work—van Gogh, undaunted, continued to paint.

In my own life, I lost touch with my creativity. After college, I attended graduate school in education, and for the next 30 years I was a teacher, organizer, and lobbyist. I channeled my imagination into home decorating and sewing. Intimidated by my early, brief success, I never painted again. I wrote a few poems but was afraid to let go, to float into the white page. To write intensively felt like entering the Tunnel of Death.

Van Gogh fully entered his painting, surrendering to the force that carried him, but his life did not nurture him. He went to Arles alone, hoping to form an artists' community in the south of France. His painting flourished—the sunflowers hung in his bedroom—and Gauguin came to join him. But the two of them fought, and when Gauguin decided to leave, Vincent sliced off his own ear.

It was a turning point that frightened him and those who knew him. He continued to paint, his works becoming even more fervent and wild—whirlwinds of cypress, blue fields, and rock. Throughout it all, van Gogh suffered episodes of emotional upheaval, and at the age of 37 he committed suicide.

Neither my father (who continued to paint) nor I (who did not) reached an emotional pitch equal to that of van Gogh, nor did we experience the tragedy of his short life. But we both fought depression. While my father was buffeted by one creative urge after another, the muzzle on my creativity did not make my life any easier. In fact, it is likely that my depression was greater because I denied my soul its voice.

I was afraid of going crazy, of entering the intense yellow light and not coming back. Carl Jung once said, "A person must pay dearly for the divine gift of creative fire." I glimpsed only one path: going into the fire, like van Gogh and my father, and being consumed by emotion. It was a choice I felt I could not make, so I hovered, uncertain, at the edges of my creative life.

I struggled to write in my waking hours, but it was my psyche that offered help. A dream appeared, unexpected:

I'm on a train crossing France. The goal is to reach London, the home of British theater and the literature I've loved for three decades. My itinerary says I will change trains in central France, but the train stops at "Aryll." I get off—it is beautiful, scintillates with sunshine and Mediterranean blue skies, but it isn't on the route to London. I decide to return to my starting point with the hope of finding a different route. On the return trip, I see a sign in English: "You cannot return to the starting place by these tracks." I take another direction, but I'm lost.

When I awoke, I knew the dream was important, but I didn't know why. Then a friend suggested that "Aryll" sounded like "Arles." Excited, I began to work with the dream's images. Because I could neither return to the beginning nor go forward to London, I focused on Arles. It was a "hot spot" in the dream, the vortex of a powerful energy calling me back. I had to face it as though it were a strong wind and find out if it was safe.

I picked up where the dream left off by writing a continuation of the story:

> *Somewhere in the heart of France, I change trains and return to Arles. From the station, struck once more by the town's brazen light, I walk to a* pension *where the concierge serves me tea and assures me it is safe to be in Arles. The older woman takes me under her wing, offering to show me the sunflowers, the night café, everything.*

After I wrote the story, I found I was no longer afraid. I felt a new confidence, a willingness to enter the light. I saw myself standing in the fields at Arles under an amber sun, the golden grasses swirling around.

Then I had another dream:

> *I'm in London, playing a part in a British play. There are many characters, men and women with British accents. When we perform the play a second time, the actors are new except for me, and because I know the whole play, I narrate and speak all the parts. Then I decide to change the script, announcing that it's time for the dance. We all go backstage for our dancing costumes, which are brightly beaded and sequined. When the man in charge of costumes hands me mine, he says, "Oh, yours is the dragon dress!" I wear the dragon, the Chinese symbol for the creative fire. I play a part, speak for all the characters, direct the play.*

Now I saw that in order to reach London, I had to go to Arles. Without immersing myself in the creative fire, I could not possibly hope to write.

Over the next few days, I felt a remarkable shift in my writing. Words flowed easily, and fear seemed to roll off my back. I purchased canvases and tubes of acrylic paint and offered my creative spirit its second, long-lost voice. I checked out books about van Gogh and reveled in his colors, as though they belonged to me.

Perusing various self-portraits, I met the cerulean blue eyes and laughed. "Vincent," I said, "I've come to join your community of artists. Show me Arles, and we'll paint together—shall we?"

Ghostly Reflections in a Backyard Pool
By Therese Keane

The pool is empty of swimmers, reflecting only the clustered variety of leaves from the shrubbery and trees surrounding it. Splotches of green jiggle over the mirrored surface, moving in time with the waves left in the water from the last swimmer—me. I first came to this Bethesda back yard more than 30 summers ago, just off the plane from Chicago.

Joe Binns' pool on that June afternoon in 1972 was filled with people from the land of Washington—lawyers, journalists, foreign service officers (or FSOs—one of many acronyms I was to learn as part of the city's lingo). Joe, the man my sister Eileen would marry two years later, owned the pool and the single-level California-style house attached to it. He was a publisher. She worked for USIA, the now-defunct United States Information Agency. Many of her colleagues were FSOs.

As I now stare at the water, ghosts of summers past appear. The pool is small by Olympic standards, about 20 feet by 30 feet. Joe would usually jump in the deep end, swim underwater from one end to the other and back again—years of practiced breath

Photo: Eileen Binns

control. One summer he hit his head doing a flip turn and suffered a pain in the neck for the rest of his life.

In 1974, Eileen married Joe and had their wedding reception—with a three-tier wedding cake made out of brie—around the pool. As the party wore on during that muggy August afternoon, the international group of wedding guests gradually began testing the water. First a timid toe was inserted. Then one article of clothing was quietly removed, later followed by another—not so quietly tossed aside. The Swedish guests took their underwear off; the Brits kept theirs on. One guest threw me in. I surfaced, temporarily blinded by the water lodged under my contact lenses. As I groped my way to the side, I heard a voice above me ask, "I say, are you all right?" I looked up and found myself staring at Dwight Makins, one of the Brits sitting at the edge of the pool. Thank heavens, it wasn't one of the Swedes.

My Irish Catholic parents from Chicago—then in their 70s—were doing their best to remain cool during the disrobing and splashing of their daughter's wedding guests. Paddy, my father, stared a bit too long at Madeleine Lundberg, a Swede doing the backstroke. "Well, it's only the human body, after all, isn't it?" my mother, Catherine, observed philosophically. I was impressed with her nonchalance.

Years later, I held my own wedding reception around this same pool. But my guests avoided the water, except for a local actress, Kerry Waters, who rolled into the pool fully clothed, and a few children who couldn't resist the cool water on that warm sunny day. Perhaps the presence of children motivated the adults to better behavior, sticking to dry land and keeping their wedding outfits on.

There were no children at Joe and Eileen's wedding. Joe felt nervous about having kids around the pool with large groups of noisy people, who may not always keep an eye on a tiny, wandering, would-be swimmer. He was proved right on one occasion. During a Sunday pool gathering, the young son of a friend was allowed to come. One of the other guests, John Wicart, was a young FSO who kept snatching flying insects and eating them. Apparently, insect delicacies were looked on favorably in whatever country he had recently been posted to. I smiled politely during his demonstration, trying not to swat any insects in his direction. Then I heard a small splash, followed by a mother's terrified scream.

The insect-eater shot into the pool and within a nanosecond emerged lifting a somewhat surprised 2-year-old, barely wet from his brief encounter with the water. Everyone, including women who had earlier veered clear of John, surrounded their hero with a new appreciation and interest in insect gastronomy.

Over the years, some poolside companions have gone. Joe succumbed to pancreatic cancer in 1990. My parents have also died. Eileen is still there, but now the pool's interior is black, which turns to midnight blue in the sun's reflection. She's also added three "wedding cake" steps to make it easier to enter and exit. The California-style house will undergo some major renovations.

Now, as the day ends, the pool's water is still. The last echoes of birdsong disappear with the setting sun. The ghosts, too, retreat as night settles over the dark blue water as it gradually fades to black.

Archeology
By Lori Carruthers

Selling my house came as a bit of surprise and shock. I don't know why; it should have been an easy decision. Recently divorced, I could not manage the expense and upkeep alone. Besides, the flow of the Cape Cod was never functional and the small rooms gave me the continual itch to remodel and expand, despite the two-story house being too big for one person.

Nonetheless, it was a difficult decision—to sell the house that once was a symbol of a bright future with my then-husband, filled with promise, high hopes, and stability. I stubbornly held on to the house months after the divorce, refusing to admit failure, struggling to reach a point of *wanting* rather than *having* to sell the house.

Little did I realize that was only the beginning of my emotional journey from past to present, as I was forced to look to my new future. On the counsel of my first realtor, I packed up wooden sculptures that potential homebuyers might find objectionable. I reluctantly hid away my treasures carefully selected over two decades of international travel, stripping my personality and past away in order to not offend. I de-cluttered and tossed old furniture, dumpster finds, and half-finished projects prior to strangers and neighbors' traipsing through bedrooms and bathrooms and peeking in closets. But in

---

Up and Down

She was standing at the bottom of the Farragut North escalator, not where beggars normally wait. A knitted wool cap listed like a beached boat on her matted hair. Oily stains puddled her overcoat. Our eyes met, but I was already being carried upward, jammed between other commuters. At the top, I turned and took the escalator back down. As I dropped a dollar into her Styrofoam cup, she looked into my face. "It's you!" she exclaimed, and broke into a radiant gap-toothed smile. "You came back!" It felt good to be remembered.

—Julia Weller

---

downsizing from a four-bedroom house with two storage sheds to a one-bedroom apartment, even one with lots of closet space, I thought I needed to keep only the essential items. My former husband chose to leave with little more than the clothes on his back and those that filled his overflowing closet.

I began to look at my possessions, carefully assembled over my adulthood, with a different eye. I have a few items from my childhood, my first teddy bear Cuddles and a silhouette portrait of me by Mrs. Lakin, my kindergarten teacher.

Much of my teenage memorabilia, including class yearbooks, had been tossed years before, after becoming moldy in my mother's damp basement. The things that I have now are gifts from friends and acquaintances or items than an adult version of me chose to complement my home and lifestyle.

I considered selling my African carvings, most collected over 15 years ago, when I was a Peace Corps Volunteer in Zaire. I went so far as to get references for a buyer, but then abruptly realized that the dollar amounts recovered would not compensate for the sentimental value. So many of my things remind me of friends and the times we shared in the parts and pieces of my past, places that no longer exist as they once were. The carved wooden bowl was a gift from an older (and richer) English gentleman who was my French classmate in the south of France, with whom I shared dinner and wine in restaurants I couldn't afford. The green wicker sewing basket that was a going-away gift from Jerry, a co-worker in San Francisco. I knew Jerry before AIDS ravaged the gay community, and I often wonder if he has survived. Another souvenir is a lumpy ceramic vase given to me by a geriatric friend who shared my love for ballet. Some people may have photo albums, and others may have songs, to refresh their memories. For me, a chipped white ceramic turtle reminds me of a fourth-grade girl and her first sweetheart.

In packing up the house I was forced to look at my possessions like a stranger cleaning out the closet of someone recently deceased. The iridescent saris bought to add romance to the bedroom window, the "his and hers" watercolor portraits and other items gathered with love to decorate the home I expected to share "until death do us part" had significance to me, though not readily apparent to the undiscerning eye. Not having children to pass these special items to, I wonder what will happen to them when I'm gone. Who will care about the clock made from seashells? And the multi-hued and obviously homemade ceramic wall hanging? And those who shared their time and their lives?

I know my life is more than just things, and I don't want to become obsessed and dominated by material possessions; however, these items from the past are still a part of my present. I will find room for them in my future.

Evening Dresses
By Julie Link Haifley

Kimberly

Olga Viso wrote, in the exhibition brochure, "*Objectifying an event in a woman's life that is fraught with contradictory emotions,* Kimberly *embodies dualities: innocence and experience, individuality and conformity, anticipation and disillusionment.*"

I first saw the work of Beverly Semmes at the Hirshhorn Museum and Sculpture Garden in 1996. Her monumental 1994 sculpture *Kimberly* comprises a huge, empty bodice of gold crushed velvet hanging on a wall with an attached "skirt" of pink organza, yards and yards of it cascading at least 30 feet onto the gallery floor. More than a dozen crushed velvet pillows—matching the bodice—punctuate the billowing piles of sheer pink fabric. I was delighted and seduced by this extravagant work of art. Its pink clouds beckoned me to lay my head on a golden pillow and float into luxurious oblivion. I smiled inwardly for I had experienced the contradictions inherent in *Kimberly.*

Sentimental Journey

My mother grew up in Tonawanda, New York, in a working class neighborhood of first-and second-generation immigrants. From the little she has told me, I gather Mom's early years were marked by dissension between her parents who later divorced, living with another family as a nanny, and leaving home by 18 to make her own way in the world. Mom trained to be a registered nurse at Michael Reese Hospital in Chicago, then joined the Army and went overseas. She met my father, a captain in the Army Corps of Engineers, at an officers' club in Ledo, Assam, India. Like many couples of that era, they danced to "Sentimental Journey," which became "their song." After the war, they returned to the States and were married in 1945 by a Justice of the Peace in St. Louis, Missouri. Dad took her "home" to Knoxville, Tennessee, where he had a tight circle of friends and a network of prominent relatives. As a "Yankee," my mother was unaware of the rigid code of Knoxville society and slow to be accepted by its matrons, despite Dad's standing in the community.

Nine years and three children later, Mom finally was invited to join the Knoxville Junior League. For her formal presentation to the League, she wore a purple strapless evening gown with a skirt of layered net falling just below her knees. She wore simple jewelry and around her shoulders a length of matching purple tulle. A photograph shows her standing in the living room of the house they had built on Kenesaw Avenue: She is 30, tall and shapely, with wavy brown hair and a generous sprinkling of freckles across her face and arms. She appears relaxed, confident, smiling with a clear gaze that says, "Yes, I've been accepted, but I am joining you on my own terms." Yet in later years, she often said she had lived there 25 years before she felt that she belonged.

Moon River

My social grooming in Knoxville began with ballroom dancing lessons during my early teens, followed by presentation at the Junior Assembly—the first of many introductions to society—in seventh grade. Perhaps because of my mother's austere upbringing, she took me to the Junior League consignment shop for my first evening gown. I was mortified to think that one of the society matrons would recognize the dress, or worse still, that one of the previous Assembly presentees had worn it first. My fears may have been unfounded, but I did not wear the dress again.

The next special occasion, an eighth-grade formal dance, found me wearing another hand-me-down. A picture of me and my date under glittery cutout letters spelling *Moon River* tells it all: I stand awkwardly next to a beanpole of a boy in a dark suit, the purple net of my mother's dress dipping well below my knees, all but hiding my calves—the only shapely part of my 14-year-old body. Mom had made two-inch straps from the matching stole to keep the dress from sliding off my girlish bust. My white-gloved Mickey Mouse hands rest gingerly on the stiff skirt while my feet are slightly apart, their dyed-to-match satin toes projecting like miniature rocket cones toward the photographer. No less martial is the gleaming helmet of my "bubble" hairdo, teased and sprayed above my reed-like neck. Undoubtedly I had spent that afternoon at the Tennessee School of Beauty, where a novice operator practiced on my hair for the price of a dollar.

My date has short hair, a narrow tie, and thick-rimmed glasses. His expression is noncommittal—narrow lips sealed shut. His right hand reaches behind me and grazes my waist. Except for his name, I have no recollection of him—how I knew him or why I invited him to the dance. *Moon River, wider than a mile*...the distance between us.

The Twist

On my 28th birthday I struggle to pull the side zipper up the bodice of Mom's faded purple dress. Sucking in my breath, I secure a hook and eye at the top and inch the zipper all the way up. Next I remove hot curlers from hair and brush it into a shiny "flip" for this special occasion. While my husband looks for a vintage sport coat in the attic, I study my reflection in our full-length mirror. A curvaceous woman in dated finery gazes back; for a self-conscious moment, she wears a ghost of my mother's confident smile.

We drive to Capitol Hill where some friends are having a '50s party, complete with disk jockey and "oldies." My husband has given me a gardenia corsage; the heavy scent surrounds me like a cloud. I wait until the last minute to put on the old purple satin shoes, then teeter into the party on his arm. There is my friend Joanie, who keeps hiking up her strapless dress, a mint green chiffon number that is too big for her. Another woman wears a pale yellow embroidered dress from her high school prom. Soon we have discarded our shoes and are dancing to the sounds of Chubby Checker, the Platters, the Everly Brothers, Ray Charles. Pastel colors swirl in the warm May air while nostalgic music drifts upward through the trees.

Painted Dresses

She wanted to [paint] an Evening Dress, a first blush dress, with puffed sleeves and tentative open arms. It would have a sweetheart neckline; its hem would dip up to a small bouquet of rosebuds. It would be a dress to break the heart. A dress for all of them who had believed in love.
        —Shelby Hearon, "Painted Dresses," 1981

The Contributors

Lori Carruthers has written nonfiction and poetry since childhood. She began taking classes at the Writer's Center in 1998 and joined the women of Stromboli Streghe in 2001. Lori currently is working on a family memoir and a weekly *haiga* (haiku and picture) journal.

Caroline Cottom, Ph.D., writes personal essays, memoir, and poetry. For the past two decades she has taught classes in creative writing, personal essay, memoir, and the creative process. She and six other alumni of the Writer's Center personal essay classes began Stromboli Streghe in 1994. Her book *The Isle of Is,* co-authored with husband Thom Cronkhite, was published in early 2006. Caroline and Thom teach meditation and lead spiritual retreats on Koro Island, Fiji, where they live with their cat Kui. Caroline can be reached at center-within@connect.com.fj.

Nancy Galbraith, a native Washingtonian, is best known as longtime manager of the Library of Congress poetry office, official seat of legendary American poets laureate and hub of the Library's public literary programs. In her avocation, art therapy, she holds an M.A. degree and a string of publications. Her career path meandered through stints at the Central Intelligence Agency, law school, and steamship travel, winding up at the Writer's Center, where she studied under Joseph Mancini and William O'Sullivan. Now 70-something, Nancy has two P.E.N. Syndicated Fiction awards.

Julie Link Haifley grew up in Knoxville, Tennessee, and moved to Washington after graduating from college. She has worked in museums, including the Textile Museum and several Smithsonian museums, for more than 25 years. She began taking courses at the Writer's Center in 2000 and plans to devote herself to writing when she retires. Her e-mail is haiflink2@aol.com.

Deborah Hefferon is an independent consultant in the fields of international education and cross-cultural communication. She has worked in more than 60 countries. Her interior journey has been illuminated by writing poetry since she was a teen and personal essays for the past decade. She looks forward to hearing from readers at DeborahHefferon@gmail.com

Therese Keane wrote, produced, and hosted radio programs for most of her career. She began writing classes in 1984 at the Writer's Center, where she met her husband and, later, the women of Stromboli Streghe. Her main writing interests are memoir and contemporary essays. Therese can be reached via e-mail: takeane@aol.com.

Ellen Maidman-Tanner has written books and articles, including a historical fantasy novel, *Days Dark as Night,* co-authored with her husband, Michael Tanner. She recently wrote a monograph for the Cato Institute, *A Community Leaders' Guide to Social Security Reform.* She is currently working on the sequel to her first novel and on a play about 9/11.

William O'Sullivan has taught the personal essay at the Writer's Center since 1993.

Maria Hogan Pereira emigrated from Ireland to the Washington, D.C., area in 1986. She is married, has two children, and runs an office- and house-cleaning business with her husband. Maria is planning to relocate to her home, County Sligo, in 2006. She also is working on a book of short stories based on life in America and Ireland.

Barbara Shine was a medical writer-editor for D.C-area consulting firms when she fell in love with the personal essay and joined the Stromboli Streghe in 1994. She now lives in Virginia's blissfully rural Northern Neck, where she writes, leads writing workshops, volunteers with a local shelter, dabbles in collage, and produces critically acclaimed cranberry-almond biscotti. Her second home is on the Web at www.bshinewrites.com.

Allyson Denise Walker has written fiction and poetry since childhood (including haikus composed in third-grade language arts class), and she has been a member of the Stromboli Streghe writers' group since 2003. She is currently attempting to set a record for the number of cups of hot chocolate a writer can consume while producing a novel. You can write to her at allyson@redbeanmedia.net.

Julia Weller has been writing stories and memoirs to entertain her family since she was a child. A journalist-turned-lawyer, Julia grew up in Germany, Belgium, and England and lived in Canada before coming to the United States. She lives in Bethesda, Maryland, with her husband and three daughters and is currently working on two novels simultaneously—a historical fiction and a teen mystery. Julia's e-mail is ojweller@gmail.com.

Itamar David Yannai is an Israeli artist and designer. He holds a degree in industrial design from the prestigious Bezalel Academy of Art and Design in Jerusalem and is currently completing his master's degree in Transportation Design at the Scola Politechnica di Design in Milan. His e-mail address is itamaryannai@gmail.com.

Publication Credits

978-0-595-41403-1
0-595-41403-6

Printed in the United States
66584LVS00005B/220-246

9 780595 414031